ALSO BY DIANA HUNT AND PAM HAIT

Studying Smart

THE TAO OF TIME

Diana Hunt, Ph.D.,
and Pam Hait

A Fireside Book
Published by Simon & Schuster
New York   London   Toronto   Sydney   Tokyo   Singapore

Fireside

Simon & Schuster Building
Rockefeller Center
1230 Avenue of the Americas
New York, New York 10020

First Fireside Edition 1991
Published by arrangement with Henry Holt & Company, Inc.
115 West 18th Street
New York, New York 10011

FIRESIDE and colophon are registered trademarks
of Simon & Schuster Inc.

Manufactured in the United States of America

1   3   5   7   9   10   8   6   4   2   Pbk.

Library of Congress Cataloging-in-Publication Data

Scharf-Hunt, Diana, date.
    The tao of time / Diana Hunt and Pam Hait.—1st Fireside ed.
      p. cm.
    "A Fireside book."
    Includes bibliographical references.
    1. Time management—Philosophy. 2. Tao. I. Hait, Pam.
II. Title.
HD69.T54H86   1991
650.1'2—dc20   90-26053
                                              CIP

ISBN 0-671-73411-3 Pbk.

TO OUR CHILDREN
*who have come into this world
with a perfect sense of time*

TO KAITLYN
*who has helped me return
to the joy of the moment*

TO HUGH
*who has taught me about
rhythms and purpose*

TO JAMIE
*who lives in the world
of synchronicity*

Of course! It's now—this very moment! The past consists of moments gone by and the future of moments to come, so neither of them could exist without the present.

Richard Ende, *Momo*

CONTENTS

Section III. The Daily Way: Old Time Tactics and New Time Challenges

Section IV. The Way of Time

ACKNOWLEDGMENTS

We would like to thank our husbands, Bob Hunt and Glen Hait, who have believed in this project and supported us throughout. Without them, our time would not be as joyful or meaningful.

We would also like to thank our agent, John Wright, who was unfailingly encouraging and calm and who had the vision to know that we really could do it.

Thank you especially to our editor, Donald Hutter, for his unerring judgment and direct insights. His advice was not only sound, it brought this project to fruition.

Finally, thank you to Martha Liefer, to the Social Venture Network, and to all the people whom we interviewed, who illustrate that you can be successful and still heed your own rhythms and follow your own pace.

INTRODUCTION

The origins of this book began with Diana's corporate experience teaching time management seminars to business and professional clients. After years of watching people in the seminars, she began to discern a definite pattern. Everyone started out enthusiastically in these classes. People were highly motivated and eager to master and use the techniques. After a period of time, however, motivation dropped off. Although Diana's clients continued to use the system she taught them, gradually they became disheartened as they realized that even this highly comprehensive time management method was not providing the freedom and control they were seeking.

Diana eventually concluded that no external system could produce the results people sought. Instead of going to an outside source, to truly manage time, she believed, we must begin from within.

Her idea lay dormant for a number of years. It was only after we collaborated on a time management book for college students and several magazine articles about children and couples and time that we began in earnest to pursue the idea of an inner time management approach. It was clear to us, from the mail we were receiving, that the definitive work on time management had yet to be written. People were not feeling comfortable with time despite all the quick fixes and techniques available to them.

As we began to work together to develop this idea, we realized that we were approaching this subject from two very different positions. Diana takes a more spiritual view; Pam is the practical voice. Rather than seeing this as a problem, we quickly realized that our collaboration was an advantage. Our method of operation never varied. First, Diana had to convince Pam that her ideas would work. Then Pam gave the ideas a "voice."

As we continued to work on this new approach, we naturally began to live the philosophy. We each began to notice changes in the other. Diana, always calm and cool, went from being an organize-everything-in-my-life-by-sections person to literally eliminating most scheduling. Today she continues to carry a three-ring binder organizer, but she uses it entirely differently. For instance, she no longer spends any time scheduling and sequencing. She uses the book mainly to write down her thoughts. "And I make a to-do list if I choose to," she says.

Pam, the frenzied, harried partner, began to appear more relaxed. She credits much of this change to her getting in touch with her natural rhythms. Although she was always cautioned to "slow down and smell the flowers," she now appreciates that she does smell them—just faster than most people do. As a result she spends far less time apologizing or feeling guilty for her naturally fast pace and more time focusing on the task at hand.

Blending classic Chinese Taoist philosophy with contemporary time management at first seemed like a radical idea. After all, the message of the Tao appears to be the antithesis of that of managed time. In the Taoist way, all things are seen to happen or exist and natural order is a given. Forcing or changing that order goes against *wu-wei,* the natural force that, the Tao teaches, should not be resisted. In classic time management, in contrast, man-made or programmed order is of the essence. "Successful" time managers are those who learn how to analyze their tasks so that they may impose a new order.

Still, the idea of melding the two continued to intrigue us. As we continued reading, researching, and thinking about this concept, we found that by extending some of the principles of the Tao to our thinking about time, a natural bridge between the two appeared. The idea of a Tao of Time was not only reasonable, it became practical.

As the project progressed, we found ready proof of the Taoist belief that events and opportunities do occur when and as they should. The waiting period between our first and second draft, for example, was a difficult time for both of us. It's never easy to tear apart a manuscript. However, when we began working on the deceleration program, we realized how powerful is the Taoist concept of wu-wei. What had been difficult in the first draft now was easier. What had seemed daunting now seemed possible.

Once we had our philosophy clearly in hand, we moved on to the writing of the book. We began thinking about who we were going to interview as examples of people who were practicing the principles described in the book. After all, no theory—no matter how well thought out—would be meaningful if we couldn't prove it. It was then that we discovered another problem. No program of inner time management and organization existed.

The interviews, however, posed another set of problems. After all, no program of inner time management and organization existed.

When Pam, the ever-anxious reporter, pointed this out, Diana, the metaphysical partner, reminded that we must "trust the river." And indeed, that trust proved itself. Within a few weeks, a chance conversation with a friend led us to a series of tapes, which in turn opened up an avenue of socially conscious entrepreneurs—many of whom belong to the Social

Venture Network, an organization of business people committed to promoting issues of social worth. One interview led to another, which led to more. Synchronicity verified.

Of course, we haven't gotten this down to perfection. Some days either or both of us falls off the track and we find ourselves whirling dangerously out of control. Still, in discovering this new way of time, we've tapped into a limitless source of comfort and support. We know now that there is always time.

In embracing each day as a new adventure and challenge, we've let go of much of the preprogramming and overscheduling we used to engage in. As a result we spend a lot less time gnashing our teeth and wringing our hands over events past and yet to come. If you truly accept the premises of New Time, you know that you must let life unfold, that you cannot control every minute of your day.

Specifically we've each learned some valuable lessons. Diana has tuned in to the power of intentional timeless nows; Pam has found a new flexibility. And we both have been gratified to discover that people other than ourselves consider fun a serious business and are practicing what we espouse in this book.

It's our pleasure to share this new way of time with each of you. We wish you a grand adventure.

SECTION I

The Meaning of Time

1

Time Management as a Life Art

Time. What is it? What meaning does it have for us? What power does it exert over our lives?

Consider your day, today. The clock radio clicked on at 6:20 A.M. The first thing you saw was the digital readout. It's what you first see each day, whether you live alone or with others. Your immediate thought every morning is "How much time do I have to get up and out?"

You dive into the shower. Minutes later you're dressing for success. You tear into the kitchen and gulp breakfast. Someone fixes lunches. Someone chases the kids out to the school bus. Dashing out the door, conversation is limited: Who'll worry about dinner, pick up the dry cleaning, and take the dog to the vet? If you live alone, your to-do list makes you wish you could hire a personal secretary. You speed to the station or squeeze onto the freeway hoping to beat the daily traffic jam.

Your race to work has begun, just as it does every Monday through Friday.

Once at your desk, phones begin ringing before you can sit down. All lines. You check your appointment book. You're needed somewhere every hour of the morning. Meetings.

3

Reports. Deadlines. Appointments. You've got two hours of work to do in forty minutes. Almost before you've downed your second cup of coffee (you need that caffeine to rev you up), the phone messages start accumulating.

Multiply this by a factor of eight to ten and you have America's average workday.

Consider your leisure time. In case you haven't noticed, most Americans work seven days a week—nights and evenings, too. Gyms to tone our bodies, self-improvement courses to tone our brains. Committees to attend or chair. Golf or tennis games to be improved. Magazines, publications, books, reports, prospectuses pile up. In an information-intensive world, the tidal wave of data threatens to engulf us. And, if you're a parent, just when you settle down to try to catch up, kids with timetables almost as taxing as yours need to be ferried to a myriad of activities.

After a frenetic working day, we schedule every millisecond until we finally collapse into bed and blearily check the clock to see just how little time we have before that same exhausting cycle begins all over again.

When did you last have a real conversation? Or a heart-to-heart visit with someone close to you? Or entertain friends—with a home-cooked meal? Think about your friendships. Notice how they exist just on the phone? When was the last time you asked someone how she was *and* stopped long enough to hear the answer? Are you worried that you and your partner don't talk anymore?

How do you feel? Shoulders tight? Stomach tense? Jaws clenched? You had crystal-clear skin as a teenager. Now you fear that your next school reunion will find you sporting adult acne. We know how to eat. We've never been better informed about nutrition, but we gulp fast food.

Anxious about your frequent amnesia? Recall a name, a book title, a phone number. It's gone. Premature aging? No. Sensory overload. We suffer from glut. Our brains fail us at our busiest times, and then with cerebral contrariness they refuse to turn off when we try to relax.

Exhausted? Feeling guilty because you haven't learned how to pace your time? Fear you're the only one who can't cram thirty-six hours into twenty-four? Perhaps it's not surprising that a runaway commercial success of this decade has been the time organizer and its many clones. America is consumed by time. It's a twentieth-century jail that has stolen our freedom. It's a life sentence without appeal. Or is it?

The pace at which the previous pages were written is the pace at which we're living. Exhaustion is our national state. Time encompasses all that we are, particularly in the United States. And yet it's amazing how little we understand about this force. While we are eager to explore other subjects that affect us so that we can better understand them and ourselves, somehow we back off when the topic is time. Rather than question its essence, we accept it as an absolute.

As children we are taught to number and measure our lives by the clock and the calendar. As adults we don't question the routine. We almost never look beyond the surface of time. Rarely do we ask deeper philosophical questions, such as who created time as we know it? Are we really bound by the twenty-four-hour day? What would happen if time stopped for us? How would our lives be if the clock and wristwatch were not the acceptable measurement of time? What would our reality be if we lived in a timeless world instead of a "time-filled" universe?

Occasionally, when we are off in the wilds or away at the beach, we accidentally encounter a timeless existence. We may realize with a start that we have totally lost track of the days. During these "off-moments," away from the pressures of work, we remove our watches and reset our bodies and minds to a cosmic time frame. We do this easily and naturally and even happily, for entering such a time warp is an adventure. Instead of checking a digital dial, we scan the sky to see how high the sun is. Instead of watching the clock, we eat meals when we are hungry. If we are camping out or staying in a remote location, we synchronize our sleeping and waking with the earth's spin on its axis. Later, when we've wrapped up these idyllic days or weeks, we're amazed at how fresh and renewed we feel.

Most of us treasure these moments away from time, but few people can imagine living this way. Real life isn't that forgiving. Back on "real time," we watch the clock. We jam our schedules. We fax and FedEx and juggle car phones. We can't waste a second. All the while we wonder: Are we doing enough? If we fall behind, we feel guilty. If we keep up, we wonder: Shouldn't we be doing more?

Because the clock has turned time from a process of nature into a commodity, not only is time a "given" in our real-life experience, it's an absolute. "Time," suggests pollster Louis Harris, charting America's rushed way of life in the *Time* cover story of April 24, 1989, "may have become the most precious commodity in the land."

Yet is it? Even in the most pragmatic Western view, time is anything but absolute. Mathematical time is different from astronomical time. Social time can be a framework of historical reference. Daylight saving time is a convenient convention. Nearly every day we deal routinely with many different types of time, depending on who we are and what we're doing. "The time of the physicist is not that of the poet," writes Larry Dossey, M.D., in *Space, Time and Medicine*. "The time of the calendar is no help in knowing when to cook potatoes, although it can tell us when to plant them. The 'time of my life' is not the same thing as the time to arrive at a party. The football official's time-out is not the same as three-quarter waltz time. The time of the mystic is not the time of the scientific investigator."

For practical purposes, we treat time as elastic. We accept

that it's a different time of day in Tokyo than in Toledo. We live concurrently in fiscal and calendar years. We say "Be there in five minutes" when we mean anytime from immediately to within half an hour. And we even take time off. We do all this confidently and casually, for stretchable time is second nature to us.

Occasionally we expand time so much we use it to hide behind. Time can be a marvelous excuse. It lets us *not* say what we really mean. We can tell ourselves that we have to rush to get off the phone rather than that we're bored by the conversation; that we only have an hour for lunch rather than that the relationship is worth only one hour of our time and there are other things we'd prefer to be doing. We tell a business associate, "I don't have time to take on your project," instead of saying honestly, "I don't want to work with you."

So why, if we're so adept at juggling definitions and dimensions of time, aren't we more at ease living with it? Whether we are twenty or eighty, we share a common fear: that the clock will tick away when we aren't looking, leaving us unfulfilled. Why do we constantly look over our shoulders, reacting to the inevitable passing of minutes and hours by alternately hoarding time and doling it out? Why, since we're surrounded by time, do we treat it as a scarce resource? Why have we never found the calm and inner peace we dream of? And why do we feel that we never really get it right?

Is this strictly an American phenomenon? Hardly. Soviet First Lady Raisa Gorbachev, whose husband rules over a nation of planned economy, alluded to this all-too-human condition in a speech she made while visiting the United States in 1987. "In our age, all of us have to work. We have professional duties. We have family duties as well as social duties. A person in the twentieth century is at a loss to distribute his or her time."

Most often we sense this loss as frustration. So we counter by looking for better management techniques. We carry notebooks that detail our day, week, and month, and keep meticulous appointment schedules, but we never feel we're in control of our time and our lives. If these systems fail us, we purchase other, more sophisticated systems and try more structured time management suggestions. We even hire professional organizers—just as we do personal trainers—to get us in timely shape. But we never seem to find the perfect scheduling solution that works for us.

Of course organizing our own time is only part of the problem we face today. We must also live and work with others, which means knowing how to operate so that we don't clash with what our mate or employer expects of us.

At some point, overstressed and undersatisfied, we throw up our hands and announce that there must be a better way.

THE ESSENCE OF TIME

The control of time is not a new issue. It has confounded many of the best minds throughout the centuries. Countless scholars from the ancient Chinese, Greeks, and Romans through to today's astrophysicists have grappled with it, and yet time remains one of the great mysteries of our universe.

What is time? Is its presence dependent on the perceiver? Or does it exist independently of anyone's notice?

Plato's curiosity was piqued by time. He questioned whether time is a measurable quantity of little times or a vast, immeasurable precreated eternity. The Greek philosopher Plotinus struggled with this issue, as well. He concluded that time was derived from the soul, actually generated as the soul moved from one experience to another.

As far back as the Bronze Age, three thousand years ago, people were obsessed with measuring time. By mapping the skies, mystics and religious leaders could set the dates of ceremonies and also predict when eclipses of the sun and moon would occur. These timely predictions enhanced their reputations.

Much later the Mayans developed an entire social culture based on time. By A.D. 300 the Mayans were using two sophisticated and amazingly accurate calendars to organize their tribal life. One calendar, which counted a 365-day year recurring in fifty-two-year cycles, dealt with everyday routine. The other, which described a year of 260 days grouped into thirteen months of twenty days each, charted the sacred or ceremonial year. This dual-calendar system was more exact than the Georgian calendar we use today.

Where philosophers once pondered, physicists—from Albert Einstein to British Lucasian Professor of Mathematics at Cambridge University Stephen Hawking—now compute. Today time is grist for science. The challenge hasn't changed; in searching for an answer to how the universe was formed, scientists still question the essence of time.

For all the mixed messages we send and receive about it, a perceived shortage of time—at a critical juncture—is certain to induce fear, anxiety, even depression. Our Western view of time—an arrow shot into eternity—is not an easy image to shake. Once time leaves our line of sight, we're conditioned to believe that it speeds on, zooming from the present into the future. Thus a sense that time flies by us is stamped into our psyches.

Yet, as any westerner who visits far-flung places with different views of time quickly learns, ours is but one image. Not only are other perceptions valid, they may be more practical.

The Tao of Time begins with the premise that in this country, we live by artificial time rules. Although we may do so innocently, sincerely believing that our scheduled, clock-driven way of time is the "right way," we fail to comprehend that ours is only one of many paths through time. For instance, we Americans pride ourselves on organization. In an effort to capture and control time, we buy into a prepackaged approach. We begin enthusiastically, eager to launch offensives against bad habits. But we soon fall back on our old ways.

Despite our best efforts, we generally fail. We organize and set priorities as the system dictates and refer frequently to a bag of timely tricks to help us get a handle on this capricious entity, but more often than not we find that the conventional methods of managing our time simply do not work.

Why? Because in today's world, classic time management techniques are no longer the answer. Industrial Age responses don't work in the Information Age. Nor will these mechanistic solutions be the answer for tomorrow's world. What is needed is an entirely new approach to time, an inside-out philosophy that focuses on the individual and his or her needs rather than on managing and organizing the many needs of others.

The motive for conventional time management sets us up for acceleration. Although the stated goal of managed time is to increase our efficiency and effectiveness, in fact, the measure of success most often is speed. Doing things better is synonymous with doing things faster so that we can do even more things efficiently and effectively. In buying into this premise, we enter a spiral of acceleration that we can never hope to master. The heart of *The Tao of Time*, in contrast, is a program of deceleration, a simple five-point plan that enables people to plot a new path through time. Unlike conventional time management methods, this approach does not involve elaborate tools, expensive systems, or time-consuming rituals. Instead, you, our readers, will learn how to use your conscious thought processes as your most powerful management tool to establish your own comfortable pace while still functioning in the real and accelerating world.

In working through *The Tao of Time*, because your mind is your ultimate organizing tool, you set your own comfortable pace. Instead of starting with external time demands—all those things that others expect and demand of you—you begin from within, concentrating on those activities that are meaningful to you. Don't worry that this approach will narrow your focus to a selfish perspective. You'll find that it will release you to concentrate more openly on the people, activities, and events to which you choose to give your time and attention.

This new method, which is rooted in classic Chinese Taoist philosophy, begins with the premise that time is limitless and highly personal, a concept that has long been accepted by Eastern philosophers. It asks that you go within yourself to establish your comfortable range of rhythms and balance. Whereas traditional time management is future oriented, to achieve deceleration you'll rediscover the magic of the *now*. Living in present time helps eliminate clock-induced stress, because instead of concentrating on your schedule, you learn to release the clock and fasten all your energies on the job at hand.

Throughout the book, visualization exercises and other techniques will help you focus your thoughts to make the most of that extraordinary tool, your mind. While it would be wonderful if we could promise you a holistic package complete with universal timetables to achieve a perfect time plan, we can't. There is no one-size-fits-all plan for time. The novelist C. S. Lewis said it best. "There is no plan because it is all plan," he observed. "There is no center because it is all center." Only you can design your own way of time.

Ultimately you will find your way of time through personal exploration and experimentation. First, you'll change your attitude toward time. Then you will understand how you can direct your thoughts to affect your actions. As you start to view each demand on your day from an internal rather than an external perspective, you will begin to disengage from the power of the clock.

This way of thinking about time involves a major philosophical shift, one that the world is ripe to accept. The more you look at how we live, the more you see that the old time barriers are rapidly disappearing. Unlimited time already is with us. Because of advances in telecommunications, the world already is running on a twenty-four-hour clock. The danger, however, is that in accepting this expanded time frame, we push ourselves harder and faster. Self-push, what Jeremy Rifkin writing in *Time Wars* calls "self-acceleration," robs us of our time, for instead of following our own rhythms, we feel compelled to dance to an ever-accelerating beat. When busyness is the measure of time, no matter how much time exists it is never enough.

The business community, in particular, is fast realizing that changes are necessary. Many corporations are aware that they need to alter how they perceive time and its relationship to personal satisfaction if they mean to remain competitive. This change of attitude is gaining wide acceptance as more businesses tabulate the economic and social implications of an unsatisfied or unfulfilled work force.

On both a corporate and personal level, then, we are beginning to understand that it is only through changing our attitudes that we may effect a lasting change in how we manage our time. If there is one underlying message in this book, it is that each of us is responsible for what happens to us during our lives. We are not victims of time. We have the ability to control our minutes and hours and days, but we must do this for ourselves. No one can solve our time problems for us. We can gain lasting comfort with our time only by organizing from the inside out, by determining first what it is that we want from our lives and then ordering our hours and days and weeks to make certain that this does, indeed, occur.

Much of our time-pressured mess is self-inflicted. More than any other society, twentieth-century Western culture has erased the ancient rhythms of the universe. In our hurry to achieve and acquire, we race through life on fast forward, ignoring our natural rhythms. If we do stop to smell the flowers, chances are we're only pausing while on the run.

As time worshippers, we outdo the Mayans. We reward those who do two things at once and set their clocks forward to avoid being late. Obsessed with minutes, we immerse ourselves in time-saving devices in a futile attempt to gain more hours—until we realize, belatedly, that we've filled those spaces with even more things to do. We race to win, but at what price? Driven by the threat of time, we wonder why we feel so empty at the end of action-filled days. As Rifkin warns, "The more efficient we try to make our lives, the more speed at which we fill in our day, the less time we have for ourselves."

Discovering that "there is always time" is what this book is all about. Once you make this connection, once you appreciate that time is inseparable from the universe and that the universe is whole and interrelated, time management becomes a lifetime art. We need to master this skill because we humans share a common heritage, a legacy of time. Scholars have suggested that this ability to discern the nature of time—to mark and measure its passing—is one of the more important faculties that distinguishes man from other creatures. Human history bears this out, for, almost since the inception of recorded time, we've relied on this measure to help us separate the sacred from the profane. Calendaring has enabled us to set aside a day of rest and segregate times of ritual from our customary routine. Time designates when dancers convene on the Hopi Indian mesas just as it delineates when the holiday season begins.

Whether our notion of time is dependent on primitive astronomical observatories or on sophisticated computers, it has long been the dominant architecture in our lives. It has enabled us to create the walls and rooms of our existence. In our rush to build, however, we've forgotten that while we have the ability to construct these walls, we also have the power to tear them down.

Before we begin the tearing down and rebuilding process, it's useful to look back first at what we've been. By knowing our past, by understanding how we've arrived at this critical juncture in time, we can better plan for our present and ensure our future. We'll begin by posing some essential questions. How did we fall from our national state of grace to become the time-pressured creatures that we are today? What is the origin of our time-driven, achievement-oriented society? When did our watches become our watchers? Above all, when did we lose our way in time?

2

Classic Theory Revisited

Somewhere along the way of Western life, we have lost our way in time. More and more, time has become a commodity, a resource to be used and hoarded, traded and exploited. Although it is difficult to pinpoint exactly when we stopped seeing time as an inside power and began to view it as an outside force, two things are certain. This transformation of time has been happening for centuries, and it has long been inexorably linked to work.

Today our perception of time is so tied to work that often how we work describes how we live. Asked "How's it going?" for instance, most people take a job inventory before they answer. If profits are up or if business is challenging, the answer is "great." If our work isn't satisfying, chances are neither is life. While families and friends are important, work is usually the first claimant on our attention—and our time. This is well substantiated by statistics: Americans spend eight to sixteen hours a day working but less than an hour in family conversations.

The more involved we are with our work, the more demands we experience on our time—demands that we feel as urgent and stressful. In our more philosophical moments we may shrug that such time pressures come with the territory. Isn't a lack of time a "given" in our society, a by-product of our own fast-paced, contemporary age?

Surprise! The roots of our time-pressured society stretch much farther back in history than you may suspect. Maybe we modern time mavens did invent time-driven schedules, but we didn't originate what we call contemporary time.

If we put a date on when Western thinking about time changed, we can safely lay the blame on the sixteenth and seventeenth centuries, the period that's generally accepted as the turning point of Western civilization. Prior to 1500, the worldview was organic. People lived in small communities and were closely tied to the land. If they thought at all about time, their perception was generally limited to what was occurring in nature and what they personally experienced. They saw the full moon; they could tell when the mare was about to foal. In such a world, day follows night. Seasons appear in order. There is literally a time to sow and a time to reap, and even more significant, these periods repeat themselves in readily identifiable patterns.

Anything that could not be explained by observation was simply taken on faith. The word of the church and the views of Aristotle, both of which supported this widely held organic concept, provided the authority to perpetuate this natural worldview.

In the organic world, time is an indigenous element. Because natural events such as the phases of the tides and the seasons are part of the ebb and flow of life, time is not sensed as an outside presence. Instead, it is part of the whole—a natural given.

It wasn't until the 1500s that this organic belief was challenged. The inquisitor was astronomer Nicolaus Copernicus. Essentially, Copernicus observed that the earth was not the center of the universe, as prevailing wisdom—and the Roman church—had long decreed, but instead was one of several bodies circling a minor star in the galaxy. Realizing that his ideas were heretical, Copernicus did not allow them to be published until after his death in 1543. When this theory was ultimately made public, the age of scientific discovery was born.

Copernicus was followed by Galileo, Bacon, and Descartes—all of whom had more questions about the natural order of life. As science challenged what had been the accepted viewpoint, the vision of the organic world became more tenuous. This change would ultimately have significant consequences for how we would perceive time.

More than anyone else, Descartes synthesized what would become the new truth. His dictum, "I think, therefore I exist," ushered in the age of radical doubt. Descartes saw reality as consisting of two separate divisions—the realm of the mind and that of matter, *res extensa*, or the extended thing. Both mind and matter, the philosopher believed, were the creation of God, who was the source of natural order and the light of reason. Although God was essential to Descartes's assumptions, reference to divine order gradually was dropped as Cartesian theory ultimately developed.

In Cartesian philosophy, the natural world is a perfect machine governed by exact mathematical laws. Time is no longer envisioned as a natural part of the universe. Rather it becomes an outside force, a foreign factor that influences "the machine." Accordingly, Descartes converted time from an inside power to an outside energizer. More than three centuries later, as we rush to stay on schedule so that we may complete our business in the proper sequence and in the allotted time, we are still struggling with the effect of his conclusions.

Descartes chose the clock as his model for humanity. It was an eminently appropriate choice. By his time—the first half of the seventeenth century—the art of clockmaking was highly perfected and the timepiece was a recognized status symbol. Only the most privileged individuals could even consider owning such an elegant machine. If time itself was not yet considered a precious resource, the timepiece was. "I consider the human body as a machine," Descartes wrote. "My thought compares a sick man and an ill-made clock with my idea of a healthy man and a well-made clock."

Centuries later Lewis Mumford, an American social critic, historian, and philosopher, would note that the clock represents the key machine of the machine age—for its influence both on technical inventions and on the habits of man.

Isaac Newton, building on Descartes's observations, described the universe as a three-dimensional space that obeyed certain laws. Newton linked space with time. He described all the changes that occurred in this physical world by identifying a separate dimension—absolute time—which he compared to a flowing stream. "Absolute, true, and mathematical time, of itself and by its own nature, flows uniformly, without regard to anything external," Newton observed.

As the world-as-a-machine replaced the organic/humanistic concept of the natural universe, the rules about how to live on earth and how to relate to time changed, as well. Since the earth was no longer a nurturing, living organism, it no longer required nurturing or protection. Where once we felt a part of nature, now we felt apart from it, free to manipulate and control the world-machine. In *The Turning Point*, physicist and author Fritjof Capra points out that this sanction to manipulate and therefore exploit nature—permission that he traces to Descartes and Newton—is a typical characteristic of Western civilizations.

As this mechanized view of nature became the norm, the organic notion of time as innate and unchangeable was eliminated entirely. What remained was time as an external measurement, a separate entity that affects both space and matter, a foreign force that can be harnessed, used, and exhausted.

TIME AND THE INDUSTRIAL AGE

By the eighteenth century, although the world-as-a-machine was accepted as the basis for scientific thought, society was still dependent on agriculture. Consequently, the organic view of work and time prevailed. Work was task oriented. If time counted at all, it was measured by the job being done. In an organic world, no one worries if it takes two hours or four to plant a field. The act of planting—not the time required to do it—is what matters.

By the 1800s, however, the work pace had quickened. The Industrial Age, which had begun in Holland and England, was spreading throughout the rest of Europe, Japan, and North America. In the United States, in particular, a land rich with immigrants, cheap labor fueled mills and factories.

At first, the advent of machines to do work that had previously been done by hand did not noticeably affect workers' perception of time. "On the contrary," states Lois Scharf, associate professor of history at Case Western Reserve University. "During the early years of the Industrial Revolution, work followed the old agrarian cycle. When the first New England mill girls went into factories, the workday and the workweek were much like they had been traditionally. You worked from sunup to sundown, longer in the summer and shorter in the winter."

But by the 1850s, the factory was imposing social and behavioral changes that were slowly being felt thoughout the workplace. If factories and mills were to operate properly, work had to be interrelated and coordinated. Tasks were organized so that they could be accomplished during set hours, at a steady pace, and in a specified order. As Scharf points out, "A new sense of work discipline developed, and it became a discipline that was time instead of task oriented."

This new work ethic was dependent on and measured almost entirely by clocks. By the mid-1850s, clocks had swept the country. Everywhere, hours were duly noted with bells and chimes. Then in 1876 the Seth Thomas Clock Company of Connecticut added something new. They invented the wind-up alarm—and waking up was never the same again.

Ticking, ringing, chiming clocks ordered people when to work, to rest, and even how and when to play. As workers learned to read hands instead of noticing sun and shadows, the natural, cyclical prompts—the sun, moon, stars, and seasons—were rendered nearly obsolete. Not only did these mechanisms revolutionize the workplace, they modified lifelong habits—both on and off the job.

By the end of the nineteenth century, clocks controlled nearly every aspect of life. The ultimate timely invention was the railroad timetable, for with it clocks not only controlled the movement of people but the flow of services and goods, as well. So essential was this tool, so pervasive its influence, that some experts insist we can trace the transformation of how we relate to time not from the appearance of mills and factories but rather to the debut of the timetable.

Even playtime was dramatically affected by the appearance of clocks. Before 1860, all games developed were open-ended. In baseball, for instance, time is not a factor. The game is still played according to innings—not according to artificial time. In contrast, most sports developed after 1860, such as basketball or football, are ruled by the clock.

TIME MEETS MOTION

At first, clocks were merely a tool to help workers establish a routine, but soon these mechanisms began to rule the labor force. Under the watchful face of the ever-present clock, the familiar, organic framework of work slowly vanished. With hours and minutes to be accounted for, time—not the task— became the focus.

In 1875 Frederick Winslow Taylor catapulted time into a new dimension. Searching for a way to increase productivity, he reasoned that if manual work could be better managed (that is, accomplished in less time), workers would be more productive. To prove his point, he adapted accepted scientific tools—research, measurement, and analysis—to examine laborers' routines. Ultimately Taylor's observations led to time and motion studies.

Like many new ideas, the concept was conceived with good intentions. But in analyzing and refining the relationship between time and motion, Taylor changed the essence of work. Before his study, workers traditionally approached jobs from a craft-oriented and therefore individual perspective. A shoemaker, for instance, never worried how long it took to cobble a shoe; what he cared about was producing a shoe of beauty and durability. What's more, how he did it was largely up to him.

Taylor introduced a time-directed, more impersonal approach. By streamlining routine—breaking tasks into predetermined sets of motions—he recognized that workers could control their time and become more productive. He also had some recommendations for the work force. Workers should talk less and work more, and concentrate more completely on the task at hand. These observations set the standard for the modern workplace. Today, as companies publish employee handbooks, debate policy, and even break for coffee, we largely have Frederick Taylor to thank.

Taylor made one serious error, however. He assumed, for the purposes of his studies, that there is only "one right way" to do a task. While this was ultimately proven false, the damage was done. Wrong or not, Taylor's conclusions about time and motion—opinions that surfaced later in time management theory—continue to haunt us. As we plan a sales strategy or organize a complex project, we often question whether or not we are doing it "right."

Until the 1930s, managing time consisted mostly of management telling labor what to do and how to do it better. Then Ivy Lee, an enterprising management consultant, had a historic dinner with Charles Schwab, who was chairman of Bethlehem Steel Company. Their conversation eventually opened a whole new field of study, one based on mental management instead of on mechanical movements.

The story goes that over dinner Schwab complained to Lee of all the things that he had to do. Schwab asked for advice on how to better manage his time.

On the back of a menu Lee wrote out instructions. Every evening Schwab was to write down the six most important tasks he had to do the next day in order of priority. Every morning he was to begin working on item one and continue until he finished it. Then he should start on item two, and so on. At the end of the day Schwab was to tear up that list— and start over.

When the steel executive asked the price of this advice, Lee suggested that Schwab use the plan for several weeks and then pay whatever he thought it was worth. Ultimately Lee received a check for $25,000—a sum representing more than $100,000 in today's money.

While Lee's advice was sound and Schwab was obviously delighted, the consultant made some questionable assumptions. For one thing, Lee assumed that whoever makes such a list has complete control over his or her time. Most of us don't. We get interrupted. Plans change. Mechanical equipment fails us. Nor did Lee consider mood swings or energy fluctuations. Some days even the most complicated tasks seem effortless, while at other times we can get bogged down by the simplest detail. Nevertheless, flaws and all, Lee's list of six was accepted as the basis for modern time management.

Despite its limitations, Lee's concept made sense for a number of reasons—not the least of which was that it was in sync with the style of the day. The crazy twenties had vanished in a cloud of ticker tape and what had emerged was a turbulent period of economic uncertainty and political upheaval. In this insecure world, people longed for control. They took solace in the familiar image of the world-as-a-machine.

In the Social Realist and Precisionist schools of art, equipment even appeared as a theme captivating audiences who saw in this artifice hope for a rational and controllable future.

EFFICIENCY ARRIVES

In 1905 Albert Einstein challenged Newtonian truth with his theory of relativity. In determining that space and time are relative concepts, intimately and inseparably connected, he forever changed the way that both are perceived. To most Americans in the early part of the twentieth century, Einstein's formulas were only chalk drawings. But with World War II and the explosion of the atomic bomb, his calculations became frighteningly real. Even so, it would be forty more years before science would fully grasp the implications of Einstein's conclusions as they relate to our perception of time.

Time management surfaced again after World War II as productivity once more became a priority. As consumers happily restocked their depression-depleted and war-rationed lives, corporate management found it had both the money and the impetus to improve efficiency. Efficiency specialists, all searching for ways to step up work performance, were only too happy to oblige.

As they dusted off Lee's list of six, which had been aimed at anyone who wished to improve their productivity, experts of the fifties added one important modification. They focused their efforts on management, with the specific intention of showing executives how to improve their use of time, particularly in their work settings.

By the early sixties, a few innovative corporate leaders were taking time management seriously. Companies whose method of operation focused on automation, such as the automobile industry, quickly grasped the significance of making optimum use of time. Next, industrial and service company executives began to put these techniques into practice. Once business gave its nod of approval, time management became a fact of corporate life.

As the corporate world converted to the concept of managed time, a pattern emerged. Organization began at the top—with key executives. Teach them to manage their time well, and the effect would trickle down throughout the system, for top brass acts as role models for those farther down the line.

Although Lee's list was practical, executives in the sixties observed that it wasn't really adequate for them. In the course of a single business day, they had more issues to deal with than could possibly be distilled into a list of six. So Edwin Bliss, a time management author, presented an alternative. He enlarged Lee's list from six to ten items—and added a new twist. Bliss recommended that every evening businessmen should write a list of ten activities they would like to do the next day. That list should include things they might not normally get around to do unless they consciously "made" time. The two items of highest priority should be scheduled with specific blocks of time in which to accomplish them. When those tasks were accomplished, the business person would move on to the other activities listed the night before, continuing to choose two priority items as long as time remained.

Bliss based his method on the statistical 80–20 rule. This rule assumes that just 20 percent of the people cause 80 percent of the total variance in a population. Accordingly, he reasoned that just 20 percent of the items in any ten-item to-do list embody 80 percent of the total importance. Thus, doing the two most important or highest-priority items out of a list of ten should let anyone accomplish 80 percent of what he or she really needs to do.

Extending this reasoning even further, Bliss offered a final, soothing note. Since this approach "assured" that you'd have accomplished 80 percent of what you needed to do by com-

pleting even two items on your list, no one ever should feel
defeated if he or she didn't finish all ten.

Not surprisingly, the 80–20 theory was enthusiastically
endorsed by a business population primed on success. Businessmen got out their pads and attacked their lists optimis-
tically. Time control was only ten items away.

If Bliss offered words of encouragement, Joseph Trickett,
the next time management expert to propose a significant
change in managing style, suggested executive euphoria.
Trickett picked up on a discrepancy in Bliss's scheme. Bliss
assumed that if you identified an item on your list as a priority,
it was. Trickett wasn't so sure. Not only did he question the
correlation between urgency and importance, he also dared
to suggest that what appears to be urgent isn't always what
is important.

To prove his theory, Trickett encouraged managers to
analyze activities carefully. He recommended that managers
make a list of all recurring activities that characterize their
job, sort that list into predetermined categories, and then
analyze each activity as to whether it was intrinsically important or urgent, could be delegated, or was part of what
Trickett called "communications."

With the analysis completed, Trickett encouraged managers to focus on the important and the urgent by analyzing
these significant activities from the company's point of view.
If you did this, you'd not only be efficient, you'd also be
effective.

In the 1960s, business eagerly took all this in. To lists, they
added analysis. Management learned the fine art of separating.
Activities were divided into categories. Tasks were dissected
and delegated. Stacks were earmarked for management or
employees' attention. Even people were rearranged into convenient groups based on how frequently managers saw or
talked with them. Everything was divided into smaller pieces
so that time could better be digested and controlled. By pre-

sorting, management was liberated from unimportant time demands and freed to concentrate on more important matters—like long-range planning. Time management experts were certain they were on the right track. The road to managed time, it seemed, was paved with categories, priorities, and planning—all based, of course, on accurate analysis.

Few people questioned how much time was consumed analyzing and subdividing. And even fewer wondered how this narrowed focus was affecting their perspective.

In 1967 Peter E. Drucker, author and well-known management consultant to business, came up with a new slant on analysis. Drucker recommended that executives should begin making decisions about their time by keeping a chronological record of everything they did on the job for a specified time, then review each activity on the list by asking three questions: What am I doing that does not have to be done? What am I doing that could be done by somebody else? What am I doing that wastes the time of others? By answering each question honestly, executives could ascertain which things they did that could be eliminated, which could be delegated, and which were time wasters.

Drucker's idea was well received by a corporate world schooled in inventory control and product analysis. Not only did this method talk the language of business, it promised a panacea—control. By the late sixties, society was reeling from social upheaval. Traditional authority was being challenged on every front. Women and minorities were clamoring for civil rights. An entire generation was rejecting established values and, in particular, the war in Vietnam. Corporate America was painfully aware that the rules were changing fast, and for the first time in the history of this country, industry was nearly powerless to respond. Gaining control over time was one way to create stability in a decade when nothing seemed certain.

In 1972 time management author and expert Alec MacKenzie expanded on the chronological time record concept. Where Drucker had suggested that you keep this time log temporarily, MacKenzie recommended that the diary become a permanent time management tool. By keeping an Executive Time Inventory, businessmen could monitor their schedules to enchance control. If the concept was time-consuming, it nevertheless forced executives to be honest about what they did all day. What's more, MacKenzie's method encouraged executives to plan their time in weekly as well as daily chunks.

Then Alan Lakein offered still another variation on the time-control theme. In his 1973 book, *How to Get Control of Your Time and Your Life*, Lakein built on Drucker's diary, which had its roots in Ivy Lee's list of six. In particular, Lakein decided that it wasn't enough merely to list all the activities you need to do. You should also label each one according to its priority. To make this easier, Lakein provided three categories. A items must be accomplished today; Bs must be done within three to five days or may be delegated. C activities, Lakein decreed, count as priority long-range items.

As the Human Potential Movement caught fire during the 1970s, it generated more steam for time management. In a world where personal realization was essential, time was of the essence. How could you make the most of yourself if you couldn't make the most of your time? One bothersome side effect was beginning to appear, however. With each successive modification, the art of managing time grew increasingly more complex. By the 1970s, even Ivy Lee would have been hard pressed to explain it quickly. What with priority groups, activities analysis, time logs, and planning techniques, an efficiency expert needed more than the back of a menu to make a point.

Even if a few skeptics were counting all the time it took to sort and stack, categorize and label, most people were sold on a subdivided world. They were so convinced, they took time management home with them. If being in control at work was good, being organized at home was even better.

The more you could cram into twenty-four hours, the more productive you would be and the better your chance for success. As eager achievers began applying the principles of goal setting and priority planning to their personal as well as professional time, the "well-balanced" executive emerged and acceleration became a subtle fact of life. Now we had defined the ideally planned, superbly organized, and tightly scheduled role model—the hypothetical perfect person who we were all supposed to aspire to be. Except we couldn't be that perfect person. The more we practiced managing time, the more we felt we had to do. And the more tightly acceleration gripped us.

SYSTEMS AND SEMINARS

During the 1960s and 1970s, some people dropped out rather than fight the time-pressured tide, but the mainstream of society plunged ahead—clutching calendars and Valium, watching clocks and their ulcers. If only we could get more organized, we could beat the clock. The corporate world responded to this sentiment with time seminars and training sessions. Some sessions concentrated only on the theory of time—why time is important in the broadest sense. Others took a more focused approach, presenting specific techniques that executives could put to use immediately. Often these how-to seminars came packaged as systems and usually included notebooks with which "graduates" could practice all their newly learned techniques. By the early 1980s there was a seminar for every type of businessperson and every corporate season.

Most corporations stressed a team approach to time, believing that if everyone pulled together to control it, the company could win the economic game. Still, for all the training and strategy, the corporate game plan didn't work. During this period, one of the major problems of the corporate world was identified as management's inability to manage time effectively.

By the 1980s a few successful, thinking individuals had begun to question whether they enjoyed being workaholics and whether they wanted to live this way for the rest of their lives. In reality, however, only the rare individual did anything about it. People had few choices if they wanted to stay on the fast track. To be successful, every moment had to count. It was a truism of life: Not only is time work, it is also money.

Consultants rallied with a corollary of that truism: If time is money, then more time is essential. Therefore, the answer in the early eighties was to build a total time system—the ultimate organizing machine that could deposit more time into your life. While there are many variations on these programs, each begins with planning, works through strategy, and promises to deliver streamlined results. Like the cogs of a well-oiled machine, each part is geared to mesh with the next, with the ultimate product being manufactured, controlled time.

But even this complete and systematic approach has failed us. Although we buy these packages hoping they will show us how to manage our time, they can't. Instead of making us more sensitive to our own time-driven needs, they make us more aware of others' time demands. We think we're buying time, but we're getting structure.

Let's take a look at how this works. You've got a list of twenty things you need to get done—phone calls to return, people to see. Using your time management skills, you separate them into categories and then subdivide these as to priority. You write these down in your organizing notebook and leave yourself a half hour for lunch. As the day progresses, however, your carefully stitched schedule threatens to unravel. Unexpected glitches occur. There are fires to be put out. You start to worry that you won't get everything done. Still, you diligently check off items as you finish them. You hardly notice that some give you pleasure—or a sense of satisfaction—while others don't. At the end of the day, you've accomplished some of what you'd intended to do—but you feel harassed that you didn't do it all. Your frustration level rises. You can't put your finger on why you feel dissatisfied. True, you worked through lunch, but that often happens. You had planned to call your tennis partner, but you tabled that. So much for scheduling a game this week.

You plan to use the weekend to unwind and find time for yourself. But on Friday, your calendar explodes. Fearful that time is getting away from you and nervous that you'll start next week behind, you use Saturday and part of Sunday to catch up. Even so, you can't relax because you promised to analyze the budget for your Rotary group and there's a meeting to attend for a charity auction.

On Monday you start all over again. The first thing that hits you that morning is remorse. As you fasten your trousers or skirt, you realize that in your flurry to stay on schedule and not disappoint anyone you forgot all about your long-range goal to get in shape. You never worked out.

We get into trouble with systems for a number of reasons, not the least of which is that they make some questionable assumptions.

From a philosophical perspective, systems strategy begins by presuming that time is finite instead of free-flowing. It does not acknowledge that the templates we lay over time—minutes, hours, days, weeks, and months—are merely convenient and traditional measuring devices invented to help us connect with time. By seeing time as limited, we put limits on ourselves, boundaries that we sense as pressure when our best-laid plans are thrown out of kilter.

Nor do time management systems, popular since the mid-1970s, encourage us to look beyond our lists. They assume that what we think we need to do is what we would choose to do if we had a choice. But we aren't asked to consider if these activities are appropriate to our nature or even if they're convenient for us at these particular moments. What we have, instead, are instructions detailing how to program these demands into our system. Once entered in our agendas, we're committed.

Time management organizers—whether bound in calfskin or ostrich, packaged in VHS or audio cassette—still are not the answer. Despite the fact that each package is planned to help us relate to time better on a daily basis through step-by-step, easy-to-follow instructions, we still aren't comfortable with time. Part of the problem is that we get mixed messages from such systems. The blank lines in organizers entice us to schedule systematically, but they also make us feel guilty if we leave too many spaces. Bigger notebooks are billed as tools we need to keep track of our busy lives. But what they really do—apart from giving us backaches—is give us more space to juggle the demands of others. Daily, weekly, and monthly deadlines are designed to steer us toward our long-range goals. But as often as not, they lock us into uncomfortable situations.

Above all, these systems don't deliver the promised results. Instead of feeling in control of time, we feel confined by our routine. We search for freedom, but we find frustration. And we don't discover more time. Inevitably we blame the system and identify time as the problem. It isn't. The problem lies within us.

Instead of condemning the system, we need to look to ourselves. This isn't easy, because time management programs rarely invite time for introspection. Once we activate the system and plot our time plan, we're urged—in fact, expected—to move ahead according to the schedule. The schedule is all-important. So we push on, allowing ourselves just seconds to stop and think, evaluate our routine, review our reactions, or consider our changing needs. Such brief moments can't provide us with the clarity we need.

After fifteen years of these time management systems, through various "improvements," it's clear that our contemporary time machines have failed. The organizer notebook may be this decade's status symbol, but time still slips away. Although we are inundated with timely advice for everything—from buying gifts to setting up subfiles to complimenting employees—few people feel that they are in control of their time.

What's wrong?

For the first time since time management techniques were introduced in the 1870s, the methodology is out of step with reality. We have entered the Information or Einsteinian Age, yet we are using time tools from the Industrial Revolution. The tidy world of the 1950s, a world where life fit into handy categories, doesn't exist anymore. Over the last thirty years, roles have blurred. The gray-flannel organization man, who was met at the door each evening by his adoring wife holding his martini (stirred, not shaken), has vanished. In his place is a thinking executive person—often a woman. A professional woman these days has multiple responsibilities and a hectic schedule. She yearns to manage her off hours and her professional time—and feel successful at both. She's figured out that being efficient isn't enough. She also needs to be effective. And she wants to feel good about herself and her accomplishments in the process. What she doesn't want to do is waste time sorting and stacking and categorizing when she knows instinctively that her life doesn't fit into those neat divisions.

The 1990s person has gone full circle—embodying both of Descartes's realms, mind and *res extensa*. We want it all— a fusing of the spiritual and the material world—and at a pace that suits us.

During the Industrial Age, it was enough to get the job done. Accomplishment was its own reward. By the midpoint of the twentieth century, getting the right job done correctly had become the goal. This change in philosophy not only assumed that there is a "right way," it implied that if only we could master methods we would arrive at a place of efficiency. But we in the Information Age are facing a far more complex challenge because we've mastered every conceivable methodology and it isn't enough. No matter how accomplished and efficient we become, we can't keep up with time today—not when it is literally being accelerated before our eyes.

The reality is that the old organization techniques we've been schooled in are incapable of handling the barrage of information that today's average person must absorb. Based on time and motion studies, these tools are geared for speed and service. They are not sensitive to individual rhythms or tuned in to who we are. So even when we stay on schedule, we feel uneasy. After we've checked off the items that we need to do, we still don't feel a sense of accomplishment or well-being. And while we create elaborate plans and pride ourselves on following through, we rarely feel that we are in control.

What's happened? What's gone wrong?

It's time to look beyond the system. Today we live in a world that is both interrelated and immediate. Almost no event anywhere in the globe goes unreported. World incidents occur and often are analyzed almost simultaneously, yet we cling to our old mechanistic methods, trying to compress time while it expands before our eyes.

Just as the clock tolled the hours, minutes, and seconds for the Industrial Age, now computers measure intervals in fleeting blips of time so infinitesimal that we cannot experience, let alone absorb, these nanoseconds. When you consider that one billion nanoseconds make up a single clock second, you can begin to appreciate the speed at which computer time travels.

No, it's not your imagination. Information is being generated faster and in ever-growing quantities. If you feel you're being inundated with data, it's because you are! Contemporary humans are exposed to more facts in a single day than medieval people faced in a lifetime. Although we've yet to realize the full implications of our accelerated culture, one thing is certain. As the clock once revolutionized work and society, the computer is reconstructing how we work and live with time.

We are now worlds away from Copernicus and Descartes, and our accelerated universe alarms us. Says a real estate broker: "What frightens me is the speed of time. I can see an event on television, and a week later there's a novel out about it. Technology makes everything much more instant, it is changing the way we solve problems and react."

The computer culture has the ability to speed us toward an essential inner journey. Because we cannot contend with the pace and mass of this artificial time-compressing mechanism, ultimately we will be forced to look beyond the "extended thing" into ourselves. In order to survive our society, we will be obliged to turn inward—decelerating, seeking time as it exists within each of us, absolute and flowing. It is a journey that is long overdue.

3

The Tao and Time

After a time of decay comes the turning point. The powerful light that has been banished returns. There is movement, but it is not brought about by force. . . . The movement is natural, arising spontaneously. For this reason the transformation of the old becomes easy. The old is discarded and the new is introduced. Both measures accord with time; therefore no harm results.

I Ching, as quoted by
Fritjof Capra

If we could stand back and see the way stretching before us as we near the end of the twentieth century, we would see two paths.

On the one hand, the nonpersonal Information Age heads straight toward space, a high-tech roadway powered by the collective scientific mind and monitored by computers. The Information Age, empowered by its technology, is a fast track of data, events, and experiences all globally connected.

In contrast, the Age of Consciousness is on a parallel path but turns into itself as it winds toward infinite space. The Age of Consciousness is intensely personal, a high-*touch* world where individuals look within themselves and realign their personal power to create their own day-to-day living experience.

For the last hundred years or more, we have been following the high-tech route. We began this journey with the Industrial Age and proved that we could, indeed, survive. However, once the machine was up and running, we began to search for more—a depth of richness, a quality of life that was lacking in our improved material existence.

It is time to rethink our present direction, to return to the two paths that reach toward space. This time we will choose the way that gives us back our inner power.

This journey has long been anticipated. In the 1920s, Charles Steinmetz, a creative engineer, who was head of General Electric's laboratories, predicted that when the history of the twentieth century is written, the greatest discoveries will not be in science but in the realm of the human spirit. In the last two decades in particular, scientists and philosophers have begun to realize that this indeed is happening. The human spirit, long ignored in favor of scientific discovery, is coming into its own. Many respected scholars have concluded that this change will be in effect by the end of the twentieth century. They are convinced that the twenty-first century marks a demarcation, a break from the ways of the past, and predict that as the century unfolds, we will see a personal transformation on a grand scale—a welling up of the human spirit—such as has never been witnessed before.

Already we are beginning to experience evidence of this transformation. In her book *The Aquarian Conspiracy*, Marilyn Ferguson chronicled the evolution of a spiritual movement and concluded that this unofficial yet extraordinary synthesis of mind and spirit has been gathering force throughout the country. More recently, in 1988, Barbara Marx Hubbard, a futurist, an author who has written extensively on personal transformational experiences, and a peace activist, created a major global event in Washington, D.C.—a peace conference that then traveled to the Soviet Union to foster understanding and accord between Soviet and American citizens. Even five years ago, such a concept would have been dismissed as a pipe dream.

Throughout the world, there has been a shift away from regional and even national thinking and a move toward attending to global needs and global thought. Fritjof Capra, author of the *Tao of Physics*, has commented on this trend, observing, "The current shift to a new world view goes hand in hand with a profound change in values." This change in values can best be described as a synthesis of mind and spirit— a fusing of the intellect and soul—inspired by a global vision.

This synthesis of the mind and spirit has been labeled the New Age. Ironically, in fact, there is nothing new about it. The philosophies that drive this movement represent a potpourri of many ancient and spiritual timeless truths that have originated from cultures other than the West. Taoism is an ideal example of this. While the New Age, like any popular movement, has suffered from hype and overexposure, the basis for its point of view remains soundly rooted in time-tested thoughts.

At heart, the New Age is about self-responsibility. While it accepts that everything happens for a reason, it also challenges us to use our own power to create changes in our existence. Above all, this New/Old philosophy exhorts us to be true to ourselves.

For the past thirty years, a diverse collection of academics, scientists, and writers have attempted to explain the growing phenomena of "consciousness" that at first was labeled the "Aquarian Age." Authors like Marilyn Ferguson and Marshall McLuhan, as well as scientists such as Fritjof Capra and Abraham Maslow, all have observed and chronicled the changes that have swept across our globe, changes that are quickly closing the gap between science and mysticism.

These changes, which the New Age not only recognizes but applauds, have extraordinary ramifications for the sequencing of events and activities that we call time. Time permeates our existence. It seeps into every moment of our lives and affects us in ways we may not even be aware of. Traditional time management has always been sensitive to the symbiotic relationship that exists between time and attitude. When we are pressured for time, we reflect this feeling as anxiety and respond negatively to whatever is taking up our time. Similarly, when we feel relaxed in terms of the time we have to complete a task or attend an event, our outlook turns positive. Unhurried, we approach appointments or jobs more openly, even eagerly.

As you read this chapter, you'll be asked to begin synthesizing your mind and spirit by opening yourself to an alternative view of the universe. This view is in harmony with the Taoist philosophy and incorporates an interpretation of time that is an extension of its principles. Although we speak of a new way, the Tao is ancient. The *Tao-te Ching*, which has been loosely translated as "The Way," is a slim volume of verse attributed to the Chinese mystic and scholar Lao-tzu. As these verses have been interpreted, to attain happiness in harmony with the Tao, one should seek a life of complete simplicity and naturalness and noninterference with the course of natural events. Written more than 2,500 years ago, the *Tao-te Ching* forms the basis for classical Chinese philosophy. Because Lao-tzu addressed his writings to a wise political ruler of China in the sixth century B.C., we can only assume that time management was not a pressing issue. Nevertheless, he wrote of a way of life in which order is part of the natural process. Order—of activities, events, and encounters—is what we usually mean when we talk about time.

Interpretation is essential to any discussion of the *Tao-te Ching*. R. L. Wing, writing in *The Tao of Power*, points out that in trying to understand a work like the Chinese classic, it is necessary to remember that Chinese characters are not representatives of words. They are symbols of ideas. Lao-tzu shows us what he thinks in symbols; he doesn't tell us in words. Therefore, Wing concludes, the work is meant to be "transmitted mind to mind, while the words are incidental to the central idea."

In today's terms, we say "Where you stand depends on where you sit." This is especially true of the *Tao-te Ching*, for this work is written on many levels. Scholars have noted that there is always another level of understanding waiting just below the level you currently comprehend. The deeper you are able to penetrate the Tao, the more personal power you develop and the stronger and more penetrating your insights.

How you arrive at an understanding of the Tao is not always easily explainable. In his book *Travels*, Michael Crichton points out that Lao-tzu says you must "accept life whole, as it is, without needing . . . to understand." While in our culture we would view this attitude as being antirational and anti-intellectual, Crichton argues that it is "another perspective, clear and consistent. Although it may not be to everyone's taste, we are obliged to acknowledge that it is a genuine solution to a genuine problem."

The essence of the Tao is that all things are One. Fundamental to this philosophy is a belief that every event that transpires within every moment is connected to a whole. Centuries later, when Swiss psychiatrist Carl Jung became convinced that the human mind does not react to causal science, he rediscovered this same concept. Jung called it "synchronicity," a term he invented to describe Lao-tzu's meaningful coincidence.

What is synchronicity? It is best described by Dr. Marie-Louis von Franz, a psychoanalyst who worked with Jung. "If you are walking along a beach and you find an old hat, two shells, a bit of wood, and an empty bottle, you might seek a causal explanation of how they got there. But the Chinese would ask, 'Why have I arrived when all of these things are together? What does it mean?' "

This notion of acausal connections—of things not easily being explained by scientific reasoning—is foreign to most westerners. We much prefer quick fixes based on logic to complex explanations involving philosophy. The Chinese cosmos, in which the universe is whole and everything that happens within one moment belongs to that whole in some way, is not our natural habitat. Yet, as you will find in the following chapters, to effect a lasting change in your approach to time it is essential that you at the very least acknowledge the validity of acausality and try to commit to being comfortable with it. Accepting acausality will enable you to become more sensitive to the presence of patterns in your life.

In the Taoist way, nothing happens randomly. Everything is interconnected. Every event occurs for a reason. Our task, as we work toward becoming evolved individuals, is to pay attention to the signals we receive and to discern the larger patterns. In Taoist teachings coincidence, what has been called God's way of remaining anonymous, is not a trick of nature. Rather it is the essence of time itself.

A journalist and human rights activist who frequently travels to war-torn countries confides that she always looks for patterns—often with the most remarkable results. She'd been buying newspapers and magazines from a small store near her New York office for months when a chance conversation set off an international chain of synchronous events. Hearing that she was going on assignment to a Mideast country, the vendor mentioned that he had been a journalist there until he had been forced to leave. He then invited her to meet a number of his friends—all of whom also had been journalists there.

He set up a dinner, and around the table the journalists opened their files and their contacts to her. Suddenly this reporter found that she was linked to the network she'd been seeking in that part of the world. "These kinds of chance things always happen to me," she says, "and I always pay attention to them."

In contrast to this belief in interconnected wholeness, the Western world divides to conquer. We compartmentalize our lives, having no sense that what we do on Sunday evening still resonates Thursday morning. For instance, on Sunday you may think about a friend who lives on the other side of the country. You haven't heard from him in months. Thursday night, the telephone rings. It's he. In the Western view, we dismiss this as a coincidence. In the Taoist tradition, the telephone call is part of a greater plan, a pattern that has been set into motion that you don't yet understand.

The Taoist way takes patience, something that most Americans are woefully short of. When it comes to time, we like action rather than contemplation. We surround ourselves with tools and time-saving devices to make things happen on cue. We Americans are a hands-on culture.

In contrast, the Tao assumes a hands-off approach. The ideal way to direct events is to employ methods that do not create resistance or elicit counterreactions. The technique to achieve a perfect flow of events is the art of wu-wei—of not working against the grain of things, of waiting for the right moment without forcing anything unduly. Instead of pushing to make things happen, in the Taoist way you wait for the right moment for events to unfold. The right moment is easily recognized. It's when actions seem to fall into place almost of their own accord. When that moment occurs, you are swept effortlessly along with time.

The ultimate goal of this Eastern philosophy is to be inner directed. Enlightened beings achieve true insight, which is defined as the ability to perceive what is correct for you in each moment of your life.

BE, DO, HAVE ... AND DECELERATE

Above all, Taoism is concerned with being. In order to achieve anything, Lao-tzu exhorts, you must first *be*. Once you have achieved being, the doing and the having follow naturally.

This relationship of being, doing, and having is also central to the primary goal of *The Tao of Time*: deceleration. When you live this concept, you achieve the ultimate understanding of your use of time. By first being the person you choose to be in regard to time—organized, flexible, relaxed—you become that person. Then the actions (doing) and rewards (having) follow naturally.

The concept of being has extraordinary power. Think for a moment how unbounded is this vital force. Being is synonymous with existence. It is both essence and spirit, nature in its most exalted form. When you choose to be the creator of your use of time, you invest yourself with natural, unlimited power. Instead of beginning with what you "have"—time crunches, deadlines, stresses, and pressures—with this new way you start from where you want to be. Being frees you to expand your perception and affect your reality.

When we approach time by beginning with be, we put ourselves in synchronicity with the universe. This is time travel in its purest form. As with a transglobal flight—when you leave the Orient in the evening and arrive in Los Angeles in the afternoon of that same day—our way of time allows us to ignore temporal conventions. Ultimately this sense of being does let us have exactly what we want to have—a sense of inner peace or satisfaction, or the euphoria of finally being at ease with time.

Of course, the Tao does not concern itself specifically with time as we westerners perceive it. Still, in countless passages—writings on natural law, living in conscious harmony with that law, and leadership—the *Tao-te Ching* speaks eloquently, however indirectly, about this force. For example, in Laotzu's observations about flexibility, he points out that those who follow the Tao know that what survives on earth is that which easily adapts to the changing circumstances in the environment. Any inflexibility in systems of belief, behavior patterns, or habits causes a negative and even destructive response.

On one level, flexibility has a direct impact on time. Being flexible allows you to respond to the moment, change plans, handle a new twist in a project, rearrange a schedule with a minimum of discomfort or delay. But on another level, flexibility triggers intuitive power. As we shift our thought patterns, checking out alternatives or switching appointments (wondering how we are going to handle all this and still make the plane), we inadvertently fine-tune our instinctive responses and reactions. At such moments we often make quick decisions that we might have agonized over at other times. We trust our instincts because we don't have time not to. Thus flexibility speeds us to arrive at conclusions that may have taken us hours or even days to reach.

In the calm light of the next day, when we review our decision and feel good about it, we gain confidence in our natural insight. Learning intentionally to trust our insight will be a Taoist-inspired "New Time" goal.

FOUR TAOIST PRINCIPLES

The term "Tao of Time" is not a translation of "*Tao-te Ching*." Rather, this new way is inspired by the Tao, specifically by four Taoist premises: those of nonresistance, individual power, center or balance, and harmony with the environment. Together these form the underpinning for the deceleration program that is described in the next section of this book.

Throughout the following chapters, we have used quotes from R. L. Wing's *Tao of Power*. Wing is a preeminent interpreter of Taoist works because he is able to explain the Tao's relevance and practicality for today's world.

While it is not necessary for you to become a Taoist scholar to absorb this new approach to time, an understanding of how these principles affect our perception of time, will help you master the concepts presented in the next four chapters.

Nonresistance

THE PATH OF LEAST RESISTANCE

Act without action; work without effort.
Taste without savoring.
Magnify the small; increase the few.
Repay ill will with kindness.

Plan the difficult when it is easy:
Handle the big where it is small.
The world's hardest work begins when it is easy;
The world's largest effort begins where it is
    small.

Evolved individuals, finally, take no great action,
And in that way the great is achieved.

Those who commit easily inspire little trust.
How easy to inspire hardness.
Therefore evolved individuals view all as difficult.
Finally they have no difficulty!

Nonresistance is poles apart from the way most of us operate with time. More often than not we work against time, hurrying to beat the clock or jam in one more activity on our calendar. We rarely wait for the proper moment or pause to discover the grain of events before deciding on a course of action. Instead, we relentlessly push on, scheduling activities according to what we perceive as priorities. Occasionally we may wonder why we feel so angry or exhausted. But we forge ahead, convinced that by imposing order, we achieve efficiency.

In contrast, when we work *with* time, when we no longer push the river or attempt to force events, we eliminate much of the effort we normally expend to make things happen.

The Tao teaches that resisting the natural flow consumes energy and concentration and drains power away from ourselves. When we do not resist, but relax and allow the experience to unfold, we retain our power. As a result, the event or encounter loses much of its ability to affect us adversely. In practicing nonresistance, we can actually reduce the critical mass of what could escalate into a crisis.

We've all encountered this phenomenon. We have a calendar so tight that one more event will send us into oblivion. The phone rings. Our appearance is requested—make that demanded—at a 6:30 P.M. reception. It's now 2:30 and we were counting on a free hour and a half to finish up loose ends at the office and enjoy a leisurely drive home before the onset of a busy evening schedule. Our reaction to this latest intrusion on our time is panic—followed by anger. From that moment on, we jealously guard each moment of the afternoon. We worry that every phone call might be an added bit of business that could further burden our already overprogrammed day.

By the time the reception hour arrives, we've done a number on ourselves. We are anxious, angry, and tense. We make it to the reception, but our attitude is so defensive that what could have been an advantageous and even pleasant time turns into an unhappy and unproductive encounter.

Had we relaxed, trusted in the right moment, and simply let the day unfold, we might have changed the outcome. Chances are, we might have completed our work in time to make a brief obligatory appearance at the reception, gone willingly instead of grudgingly, and left a far better impression. Certainly we would have changed our outlook and we would have avoided expending hours of negative energy.

Individual Power

DIRECTING THE POWER

The Tao in nature is like a bow that is stretched.
The top is pulled down, the bottom is raised up.
What is excessive is reduced, what is insufficient is
*   supplemented.*

The Tao in nature reduces the excessive,
and supplements the insufficient.
The Tao in man is not so:
He reduces the insufficient,
Because he serves the excessive.

Who then can use excess to serve the world?
Those who possess the Tao.
Therefore evolved individuals
act without expectation,
succeed without taking credit, and have no desire to
  display their excellence.

To trust in time, to know that the right moment will occur, takes a leap of faith. Lao-tzu believed that each of us is equipped with the energy to make that leap because he recognized a latent power (*te*) that exists in each individual. This power emerges when we become aware of and aligned with the life force (*tao*). We activate our power when we drop our preconceived ideas and methods that limit growth and connect with the life force. Instead of depending solely on logic and intellect, the Tao exhorts us to trust our instincts and believe in our perceptions. Thus we are able to plug into this extraordinary energy source.

In trusting intuition, we balance intellectual knowledge. This fusing of the mind and spirit enables us to build a spiritual bridge, a span that ultimately leads to simplicity.

Simplicity, as described in the *Tao-te Ching*, is the highest expression of personal power. A cosmic streamlining device, it enables us to strip away the extraneous details that often cloud our decisions. As we do, we see issues with clarity.

We've all had some experience with this. Troubled by a confrontation we know we must have with an employee— her performance has been deteriorating—we become increasingly upset each time we think about having to face her. We fear that she'll be angry, and if she quits, we'll be out an assistant and then what will we do? Finally, after agonizing about the coming meeting, we manage to pull back and analyze the problem. Relaxed, and with our ego removed to a safer distance, we suddenly see that the real issue isn't her spelling or her chronic lateness. Those are just symptoms of a more central problem: She isn't challenged by her job. If we deal with that problem, that issue, we'll not only solve the minor problems, we'll gain a more valuable employee. What had seemed impossible, now, with clarity, seems simple.

Think of clarity as the ah-ha phenomenon, that flash of insight that comes when you finally grasp the essence of a situation. By taking your individual power, giving yourself permission to step back and look at an issue, you invite clarity and promote a feeling of ease. With ease, what had been difficult now appears effortless.

Too often in our rush to achieve and stay on schedule, we experience clarity only after a situation has passed. Then we think how we would have done things differently had we been "thinking straight" at the time. Usually these thoughts point to an easier way to have accomplished a job or a more comfortable approach to what turned out to be an unpleasant encounter.

Not only does clarity make life easier, it makes us more efficient. When we consciously cut through extraneous activities and emotions and focus on the heart of the issue rather than allow ourselves to be sidetracked by secondary thoughts and worries, we streamline our reactions and responses. In turn, streamlining releases our personal power, which we sense as more control over our time and our lives.

Balance

GAINING ONENESS

Those who know do not speak.
Those who speak do not know.

Block the passages.
Close the door.

Blunt the sharpness.
Untie the tangles.
Harmonize the brightness.
Identify with the ways of the world.

This is called Profound Identification.
It cannot be gained through attachment.
It cannot be gained through detachment.
It cannot be gained through advantage.
It cannot be gained through disadvantage.
It cannot be gained through esteem.
It cannot be gained through humility.
Hence it is the treasure of the world.

Finding your center or balance is the third Taoist premise. Again, this principle is not foreign to us. We all seek balance. But we seek it in artificial ways.

How does this work? Most of us plan a day using an organizer of some sort. Traditional time management techniques have taught us that a balanced schedule should include personal and professional activities. So with this in mind, we start the day with an hour of exercise. After we shower and dress, we're off to work.

The day is filled with meetings, telephone conversations, project planning, and endless interruptions. We plunge ahead. We want to keep on schedule.

Right after work we stop off at the chamber of commerce. Then there's a fund-raising meeting we must attend. Rushed, we eat a quick dinner. Then it's off to our son's basketball game. During this flurry of activity, at times we have a nagging sense of discomfort or unease. Does balance have to be so exhausting?

What's happened here is that we've bought the artificial definition of balance. We're obsessed with doing it all—every day. We forget about our inner needs. We don't listen to our inner voice. We proceed on automatic because we think that this is the "natural" way to balance. We handle our lives as if we are following a recipe. If we combine specified amounts of work, personal, and civic-related time within our imposed twenty-four-hour day, we'll concoct that magic elixir of a "perfectly balanced life."

When we adopt a Taoist approach, we find our real natural center. We begin to listen to our inner cues and, as we act on them, we find—miraculously—that the universe supports our actions. Yet it's not miraculous. It's natural, for in planning from the inside out, you rediscover your natural rhythms. You eliminate the feeling that you're constantly in a tug of war with your schedule. Instead, as you sense your rhythm, you and your day synchronize. Just as a harmonic piece of music is off-balance when a discordant note resounds, so your day can be inharmonious when you ignore your rhythms.

Harmony with the Environment

NATURE'S WAY

Those bold in daring will die;
Those bold in not daring will survive.
Of these two, either may benefit or harm.

Nature decides which is evil.
But who can know why?
Even evolved individuals regard this as difficult.

The Tao in Nature.
Does not contend,
yet skillfully triumphs.
Does not speak,
yet skillfully responds.
Does not summon,
and yet attracts.
Does not hasten,
yet skillfully designs.

Nature's network is vast, so vast.
Its mesh is coarse, yet nothing slips through.

The fourth premise of the Tao, harmony with the environment, also has its counterpoint in time. Just as we perceive time as days and hours and minutes, Tao is revealed as it is reflected in the physical and spiritual world—in a chain of events, in the evolution of social transformations, and in the realm of ideas.

The Tao teaches that when we look within ourselves, we will find all that we need for fulfillment in our lives. But first we must have the courage to trust our inner voice and acknowledge that we are the source of our own power. Our internal understanding of power, whether it is an awareness of inner strength or a feeling of powerlessness, is completely the result of what we perceive as our environment. Just as we can "make" time or "run out of it," we have the choice to manufacture or destroy our power.

For example, if we insist that we do not have the capacity to change an unhappy relationship at home or a situation at work that is causing us stress, this belief will activate the internal processes that will assure our prophecy becomes fact. If we determine, however, that we can alter our destiny and allow our inner energy to expand, our perception of power will enable us to make the necessary changes.

As you practice this Taoist way of time, you will become intimate with your inner voice. Listening to it, trusting your instincts, you will gain a perspective on how to balance the events in your day. Discovering your inner balance will free you to live more easily in the moment. Centered, you will find that you are no longer gripped by past guilt or frozen with fear of the future. Because you are unencumbered by excessive worries about past actions or future choices, you can simplify your life.

Finally, as you become comfortable with the Taoist concept and rediscover your natural rhythms, you will find that the tyranny of clocks and schedules cannot control you. Clocks and calendars are artificial measurements, tools rather than absolutes. The only absolute in this new way of time is you.

As you gather your power and begin to follow this way

of time, you will come to know time for what it is—an unlimited flow of limitless energy.

The first Taoist premise of nonresistance gives us permission to let go of our prepackaged approach to time management. Instead of "manipulating time," we pull back and allow events to unfold naturally. With the second premise, individual power, we assert our right to direct our own time. The third premise, balance, teaches us to be aware of our own rhythms and alerts us when we are out of control. The final principle, harmony with the environment, puts us in touch with the grand scheme of life and time. It does this by speaking to us of the organic nature of this force and reminds us that we are not separate from time. Rather time is part of us, intrinsic, a given.

Interpreting the Tao in this manner gives us "permission" to decelerate, to determine our own way of time. Although it is an ancient path, because it is inner directed, the message is timeless. At once contemplative and action oriented, it is adaptable to every pace and rhythm of life.

"If we possess our way of life, we can put up with almost any 'how,' " wrote Nietzsche. During the past hundred years, we've concentrated on the hows of time. It's now time to explore the way.

SECTION II

The Way of Deceleration: A Five-Part Program

4

Before You Begin

In the next four chapters we will take you through a highly specific five-part program that will help you change the way you think about and use your time. We call it a deceleration program because only through conscious effort to counter the accelerating influences of our Information Age can we readjust the way we perceive and live with time. The six-week program comprises a series of exercises designed to help you slow down and examine your approach to daily routine. Various techniques are included to encourage you to release your time-driven attitudes by lessening the importance of clock time and increasing your reliance on Inner—your own innate sense of—Time.

The program isn't magical or complicated, but it does require your firm commitment to learn it and use it consciously. To begin with, you'll need to set aside specific times each day—morning and evening—to practice the techniques. Early morning, before you get involved in your day, and late evening just before you go to sleep (and take the experience into your unconscious dream life) are the best times for changing behavior, because these are the times we're able to focus most completely, free from outside influence and interruption.

At first the program may seem alien to you, somehow strange or unnatural, but as you become familiar with the techniques you'll be able to do the exercises easily and quickly. What's more, as deceleration becomes a habit, you'll naturally ease up on your practice sessions. Eventually you'll enjoy creating your own techniques to ease you over tough spots with daily time.

No matter how expert you become at deceleration, expect some difficult moments. Remember: We live in a speed-driven culture, a world where the "acceleration syndrome" is a recognized characteristic for type-A personalities, those driven to achieve. That's why our "Tao of Time" program includes both a strategic deceleration program (section two) and specific tactical applications (section three). The tactical exercises are aimed at helping you handle troublesome, common time problems like procrastination, deadlines, or over-programming. By using both the strategic and tactical techniques, you'll discover that you can move away from clock time but still function in a twenty-four-hour world that's filled with people who don't yet share your expanded view of time.

The new time tool to make all this happen is *visual imagery*. Many books have been written on this subject, but Shakti Gawain's *Creative Visualization* is outstanding. If you are not familiar with visualization, you may want to read more about it. A suggested reading list is included at the end of this chapter. This concept and method, also called "guided imagery," combines mental energy with affirmation. Put another way, visualization activates mental energy. It allows you to harness your imagination so that your creative powers perform the most difficult work for you. You intentionally create whatever it is you want in your life.

All of us use visual imagery whether or not we are aware of it. Usually we do it without thinking about it. We may be working on an assignment and suddenly "see" the solution. Or, while waiting for an unpleasant phone call, we "rehearse" the upcoming conversation. With this program, you'll direct visual imagery to design a new way of time.

Four factors need to be present for visual imagery to work. You must have the intent to make a change, the desire to follow through with that intent, the belief that you can make this happen, and total acceptance of the result.

If you're reading this book, you already are ahead. You obviously do intend to change the way you're managing your time. More than likely you feel plagued by disorganization and things never going the way you plan, so you've decided that *now* is the time to make changes. Although you've probably made other attempts at changing your time habits, now your desire to alter your approach to time is greater than your fear of change or your worry about any temporary discomfort you'll experience while switching habits. This time you *know* you can do it. So you give yourself the acid test. Ask yourself, "Am I completely willing to let go of comfortable but inefficient time habits to make this change?" If you answer "yes," you can be certain that all four factors—intent, desire, belief, and acceptance—are in place. If you hesitate or can't honestly say "yes," you should reassess your original intent. If you're not ready to let go of your old habits, you won't be successful in forming new ones.

WHAT IS VISUAL IMAGERY?

Many people are stumped by the concept of visualization. Don't be put off by the word. Although the term implies "seeing" something, you *can* visualize without pictures or sound. Each of us visualizes differently. Some people actually do "see" images. They "turn on" their mental VCRs and tapes begin to run. Others get audio signals when they activate visualization. They talk themselves through an upcoming situation (alone or with a close friend). And still other people visualize through "feelings," as an emotional response they receive when they think about an upcoming event or experience. As long as your receiving system works for you and is comfortable, relax. You're on track.

Know, too, that there are two different modes of visual imagery—the receptive and the active mode. In the receptive mode, we simply relax and allow images or impressions to come to us without consciously selecting the details. Says Michael Russell, founder and CEO of American City Business Journals, "I use visual imagery every day to cleanse my mind. I just see 'it' happen. If you believe it, it happens. Period." Russell, who built his Kansas City–based publishing chain into twenty-one newspapers, confides that visualization has always been a part of his life. "I thought everybody did it."

In contrast, in the active mode, we consciously choose and create what we wish to see or imagine. For example, if we were to visualize in the receptive mode about an important sales meeting, we might focus on feeling a sense of satisfaction or well-being that follows a successful meeting. If we visualize this event in the active mode, we would set the stage carefully. We would picture the room in fine detail. We would notice what everyone is wearing and hear conversations in detail. Active visualization is nourished by a wealth of detail.

Initially, the exercises presented in this program are all in the active mode because this is the easiest way to begin using visual imagery. With active visualization, you participate intentionally. Basically, you write the script the way you want it to happen. You set the scene and direct the action. After practicing active visual imagery for a while, however, you'll begin to listen to more and more of your inner messages. Gradually the visual imagery will switch from active to receptive. Receptive visualization acts like a creative shorthand. By focusing on the feelings and the outcome you want to experience from a meeting, appointment, or confrontation, you skip over the details and center on the result you want to attain.

The deceleration program described in the next five chapters incorporates all the points essential to any successful visual imagery. For the next few weeks you will be asked to:

1. Commit to using visual imagery twice a day. Set aside a specific fifteen-minute period in the morning for relaxation and visual imagery exercises. Spend another fifteen minutes in the evening, preferably right before you go to sleep, to relax and visualize again.

2. Set your goal. Decide what you want to be, do, or have.

3. Create a clear idea or picture of the situation exactly as you want it to happen.

4. Focus often on the idea, feeling, or mental picture. In addition to your specific meditation periods, bring the idea or picture to mind during the day.

5. Give the idea, feeling, or mental image positive energy. As you think about your goal, make strong positive statements to yourself—that the goal exists, that it has come to be or is now coming to you. See yourself achieving your goal. These positive statements are called *affirmations* because they affirm what you know to be true. Affirmations help you feel that what you desire is real and attainable.

Affirmations are essential to successful visual imagery because they are a way of "making firm" that which you are imagining. Affirmations fix a feeling in your mind and heart. Some people describe them as "self-talk," and in truth affirmations do show us how to talk positively to ourselves. We replace negative thinking with positive and therefore more useful ideas and concepts.

Affirmations come in many forms. They can be done loudly, whispered, or expressed silently. Some people prefer to write them down. Others even sing or chant them. There's no specific language you need to learn. Affirmations can be general, as in "I am an on-time person." Or they can be specific, as in "My report is complete for Thursday." The only requirement is that they must be stated positively and in the present tense, as if you are already experiencing the effect. They don't need to be lofty or poetic. They must only be heartfelt. A New Time affirmation, for instance, could be, "I am relaxed and centered. I have plenty of time for everything."

AFFIRMATION CHECKLIST

1. Always phrase an affirmation in the present tense as if it already exists.
2. Phrase your statement positively. Affirm what you want, not what you don't want.
3. The shorter and simpler the affirmation, the more effective it will be. The best kind of affirmation is a clear statement that conveys a strong feeling.
4. Choose affirmations that feel right to you. Don't try to force feelings or situations. When you practice affirmations, you are creating something new and fresh. The statements are not meant to contradict or change your feelings. Rather, they help you create a new point of view.
5. Try to keep affirmations fresh. Memorizing or saying them by rote can diminish the power of the statement. Think about what you are saying. Feel that you have the power to create that reality.

GETTING STUCK

All of this sounds easy enough. And it is, as long as it works. However, sometimes we get stuck. No matter how hard we try to use visual imagery, our thoughts remain blocked. Although we know we should be concentrating on how to get unblocked, instead we get more frustrated.

Blocks are usually caused by repressed emotions of fear, guilt, resentment, or anger. Any one of these will cause us to shut down. Getting past a block requires a concerted, conscious effort.

Usually we can remove the block by facing the emotion that is causing it. To do this, we must experience the emotion we have locked up inside ourselves but in a loving, accepting way ("loving" because, for better or worse, it is a part of us, and anger or frustration at ourselves is hardly conducive to unblocking). Once we face and accept the negative emotion, we allow the block to begin to dissolve. Without the block in the way, we can see through to the negative beliefs that cause the block to happen in the first place. Once we achieve that insight, we're on our way to ridding ourselves of that problem.

Identifying the constrictive belief and accepting your feelings about it are the secrets to dissolving a mental block. Understanding and accepting yourself and your feelings allows the clearing process to begin. To do this you must first love and accept yourself for having this belief and, at the same time, understand that you're ready to let go of it because that belief is limiting, destructive, and self-defeating. We all have such blocks that occur with regard to time. Otherwise we would have already overcome our problems!

Some common beliefs that create time blocks are:

Time is my enemy.
The world doesn't work according to my time schedule and never will.
There's never enough time, money, love, etc., to go around.
I don't have control over what happens to me.
I can't slow down because everybody is depending on me.

As you practice decelerating, you'll experience periods when you feel frustrated or unable to reach your goal. The following chapters include clearing exercises with each deceleration step for those times when you get stuck.

VISUAL IMAGERY AND THE TAO

At first you may not see how the philosophy of the Tao fits with visual imagery. The Taoist approach of living in the now and letting go of attachments and desires appears to be the antithesis of setting goals and creating what you want. For instance, with the Taoist approach, we're told to relax and "trust the river," yet visual imagery encourages us to take charge and set our own course.

In fact, visual imagery complements the Taoist view in three important ways. First, it affirms the relationship of being, doing, and having introduced in chapter 3. When we use visual imagery to readjust our sense of time, we reestablish a comfortable pace and thus give ourselves permission to get back in touch with who we are—with our own sense of being. When you're in touch with your *being*, you know what to *do*. *Having* then follows naturally. Visual imagery may be thought of as the first step in the journey to disconnect us from the perception we hold of ourselves in the outside world and to connect to our inner selves—to discover the power of being in the Taoist sense. By connecting, understanding the Tao becomes possible.

Second, implicit in such connecting is our willingness to release old images we may have of ourselves, visions that may not accurately reflect who we really are. This releasing is, after all, a form of letting go, which is another Taoist-derived premise necessary for deceleration.

Third, because deceleration, as achieved by Taoist-inspired teachings, occurs easily, it illustrates the presence of wu-wei. Although following this program will take commitment on your part, you will not feel forced or stressed as you change your approach to time. Indeed, you'll feel exhilarated as you liberate yourself from the tyranny of the clock. If, at any time during deceleration, you feel that you are trying to force or push something that does not want to happen, stop and reassess your intent concerning the time problem. Negative signals indicate that you're going against the premise of wu-wei.

WITH THE DECELERATION PROGRAM YOU WILL:

1. Refocus yourself in time by releasing time-driven attitudes through visual imagery and affirmations.
2. Begin the transformation to see time as a timeless state comprised of meaningful coincidence rather than a mechanical, clock-dependent entity.
3. Understand that there is no destination in time. The journey is the process.

If you are interested in learning more about visual imagery techniques, this suggested reading list may prove helpful.

Allen, Marcus. *Tantra for the West—A Guide to Personal Freedom.* Mill Valley, CA: Whatever Publishing, 1981.

Allen, Marcus, and Shakti Gawain. *Reunion: Tools for Transformation.* Mill Valley, CA: Whatever Publishing, 1978.

Borysenko, Joan. *Minding the Body, Mending the Mind.* New York: Addison Wesley, 1987.

Gawain, Shakti. *Creative Visualization.* New York: Bantam, 1982.

Levine, Steven. *A Gradual Awakening.* Garden City, NY: Anchor Press/Doubleday, 1979.

Roberts, Jane. *The Nature of Personal Reality.* Englewood Cliffs, NJ: Prentice-Hall, 1974.

Silva, Jose, and Philip Miele. *The Silva Mind Control Method.* New York: Simon and Schuster, 1977.

Spangler, David. *Manifestation.* The Park, Forres, Moray, Scotland: The Findhorn Foundation. (Out of print.)

TAPES

Bernoff, Jon, and Marcus Allen. *Breathe, the Art of Relaxation*. Manhasset, NY: Vital Body Marketing Company. *An instrumental musical journey*.

Gawain, Shakti. *Creative Visualization*. Mill Valley, CA: Whatever Publishing. *A 60-minute cassette for relaxation and preparing for visualization*.

Jones, Michael. *After the Rain*. Milwaukee: Nevada Publishing.

Rowland, Mike. *The Fairy Ring*. Milwaukee: Sonia Gaia Productions.

5

Week One:
Living in the Now

THE MESSAGE OF THE TAO:
Letting go

You need to trust in the river to know that the river exists.

The Tao teaches that we need to "trust the river." Every experience, planned or unplanned, has the potential to build our trust. Through experience, we come to realize that events do transpire as they should.

When we trust in the river, we mentally and physically let go. We release our need to force or control the flow of activities. Secure in the knowledge that the river flows as it should, we run with events rather than resist them.

To trust in the river by releasing unnecessary scheduling shifts our focus from time to task. Just as the Tao is not driven by time, the clock need not dictate how we move from moment to moment. In discovering the power of the present, we free ourselves from the demands of the clock. Trusting in the moment, we release the pressure of time.

Key Time Phrase:
There is no other moment in time but that which is happening now.
Key Time Issue:
In immersing ourselves in the now moment, we discover

the joy of concentrating on the task; we are not absorbed with time.

Inner Time Result:

Now moments release unnecessary scheduling.

Inner Time Technique:

Creating now moments through intentional timelessness.

For this week of the program, you will be discovering the power of the now moment. If you stop to think about how you use your time, more than likely much of your waking hours are directed ahead and behind you. Because you haven't learned to trust the river, you don't give yourself easily to the present. Instead of experiencing the richness of the now, you spend it worrying about the past or planning for the future—especially planning for the future, because that's where you've been conditioned to be rewarded.

When we live in the now and are totally absorbed by the activity at hand, we become our most positive and productive selves. Zooming in on the present, eliminating extraneous mind clutter, we forget about whom we must call or what job we've got to tackle next. Unrestrained by time, we focus all our concentration on the task before us, whether that task is to negotiate a tricky mogul on a ski slope or seal a contract for a business deal. Engrossed in the now, we slip effortlessly into a no-boundary place in time and space, a timeless dimension where energy abounds and time is irrelevant. During these exhilarating experiences, we may suddenly understand that *there really is no other moment in time but that which is happening right now.*

We have all touched the timeless. We've known an expanded moment during an embrace with a loved one, or when we've been immersed in a sunset, absorbed by an exciting book, or have just learned to do something for the first time. For these intense encounters, we exist completely in the present. Afterward, refreshed and uplifted, we may marvel at all we accomplished and how good we feel. Search as we will when the experience has passed, we cannot say when it began or ended. All we know for certain is that the template of clock time is useless to measure the physical or spiritual mass of such a timeless present.

How do we generate this exhilarating power in our day? By immersing ourselves in now moments—discovering the joy of concentrating on the task instead of time. The power of timelessness becomes part of everyday life.

Intentional timelessness is the technique you will use to shift your focus from time to task. As you begin to build intentional now moments into your day, you'll see that you can release unnecessary scheduling. The concept isn't mystical or difficult to grasp. In his book *Creativity in Business*, Stanford professor Michael Ray describes this phenomenon that Buddhists call mindfulness. "If you pay attention at every moment, you form a new relationship to time. . . . In some magical way, by slowing down, you become more efficient, productive, and energetic, focusing without distraction directly on the task in front of you. Not only do you become immersed in the moment, you become that moment."

In the most practical sense, now moments are the highlights of your day. They are the rockets you deploy to move through time and space as you adjust your attitude toward time. By focusing on these highlights, actually "seeing" yourself accomplishing your most important activities without the limits of the clock, you shift your concentration from time to activity. Each time you rehearse a now moment, visualizing a significant activity occurring without a specific time frame and then immersing yourself in that experience as it takes place, you reinforce your power to trust the present. Trusting the river encourages you to rely more on your innate sense of order and less on outer or conventional scheduling. As a result, much of the tension of time—the negative pressure we put on ourselves—is eliminated. Fears that drive acceleration—not finishing on time, having unfinished business left at the end of the day, and never getting to the most important things—are defused by releasing unnecessary scheduling through living in the now.

How do you recognize now moments? Although more enlightened people might insist that every moment is a "now moment," in fact we don't register each experience with equal intensity. For deceleration purposes, now moments are the most important events *you* want to experience in a given day. You may have an office full of clients to see, correspondence to complete, an important meeting to attend in the late afternoon, and a desk full of bills that must be paid that evening at home. Traditional time management urges you to set your priorities in order of consequence, doing first what *most* needs to be done. This usually turns out to be those jobs that others are depending on you to accomplish.

As you begin working with this program, you may be surprised to discover timeless nows aren't always your conventional time-managed top priorities. When asked to visualize the highlights of your typical day, you may see yourself meeting with clients or completing correspondence. Or an image of yourself sitting at your desk at home paying the household bills could surface. The latter visualization wouldn't mean that you won't hate meeting with clients or completing your correspondence. Rather, this visual clue would tell you that no matter what you accomplish in the course of a day, you won't feel satisfied unless the checks are written that night!

This first week you'll learn how to use these projected highlights to help you release unnecessary scheduling. Traditionally, scheduling is the step that clinches action. Once we schedule something, we give it power. In reality, when we tie an activity to a specific time, we often take power away from ourselves and give it to the clock. Having scheduled an apppointment or decided on a deadline for a project, we may worry more about getting that task done within the specific time frame than about completing the task itself. If you keep one eye on the clock, how can you be fully engrossed in what you're doing? This shift in focus is what robs us of a total experience.

The Inner Time technique of intentional timelessness gives you permission to retain your power. By visualizing your most important activities happening without the clock, *you* maintain control. You override the scheduling step because instead of depending on a manufactured timetable, you activate intent, desire, belief, and acceptance to empower your "nows." In a real sense, when you plug into the power of the present, intentional timelessness takes you beyond conventional time. The more comfortable you become with clockless nows, the closer you'll move toward your ultimate goal of eliminating unnecessary time-induced pressure altogether.

Some scheduling, of course, is unavoidable. If you are supposed to meet someone at three o'clock, strolling in forgetfully at two or four is counterproductive. When other people are depending on you, adhering to a schedule is not only polite, it's often the only way you can conduct business. However, it's just as true that we schedule indiscriminately. Does it really matter when you go to the shoemaker so long as you get there during shop hours? Couldn't a phone call suffice instead of a scheduled meeting? Many errands, conversations, and tasks that are simply less important don't require a time slot. We schedule these out of habit. That's why the first week of the program is aimed at breaking the overscheduling habit by creating more intentional now moments in our day.

The directions that follow are only a starting point. This first week of deceleration is designed to make you more aware of time. Although you'll practice the following technique for a week and then move on to the next step of the program, you'll often refer back to this week's step. Don't expect to perfect this exercise during the first week. As long as you practice the exercise, you'll become more aware of time.

While you are learning this step, highlight one to three

intentional timeless nows in your day. As you become comfortable with this concept, you may add more highlights. Ultimately, as deceleration becomes natural for you, you will decide on the blend of intentional nows and routine experiences that is right for you.

And as a final general point, be sure to read the rest of this chapter, ponder it, perhaps even review it, before actually undertaking the exercise. The same caution applies to each new week of the remaining chapters in this section.

CREATING INTENTIONAL NOWS

All right, let's begin altering your way of time. Set aside fifteen minutes early in the morning (preferably soon after rising) and again in the evening (preferably just before you go to sleep). Pick a place where you feel relaxed and are fairly certain that you won't be interrupted. Many people find that visualization works best for them if they are seated in a comfortable chair with both feet on the floor and the spine straight and balanced. Keeping the spine straight helps energy to flow within your body and makes it easier to experience deep relaxation.

You begin the exercise with visual relaxation. If you have a favorite meditative technique that works for you, use it. If not, follow this simple procedure.

Close your eyes and relax. Visualize the number 5. As you focus on the number, let it fade. Then bring it up again. Fade and re-create the number 5 two more times.

Repeat this process with the numbers 4, 3, 2, and 1.

After you have visualized the number 1, see yourself standing in front of that 1. Now feel the 1 being absorbed into your body.

Experience this feeling with as much detail as possible. Imagine the 1 moving through your body and slowly disappearing until only the vision of you is left.

If you do not yet feel completely relaxed, repeat this exercise.

Once relaxed, you're ready to begin identifying the now moments in your day. Your goal for this week is to let go of *unnecessary* clock-driven scheduling by focusing on intentional timeless nows. As you create them, it's important that you always visualize these experiences without the structure of the clock.

1. Create a visual image of the highlights of your anticipated day (for the morning exercise) exactly as you desire them. If you need to refer to your appointment book or to-do list to see what you have planned, by all means do so. Some people find that it's easier to run through the morning, afternoon, and evening activities they have planned and allow the highlights to surface. Others identify the most important events or activities by imagining the feeling they desire to experience at the end of the day and letting the events emerge from this focal point. Of course, all of us have days that are busier than others, but even as you consider the now moments of busier days, you'll rarely find more than two or three highlights emerging.

2. For the first three days of this first week, select one highlight to focus on. Later in the week, as you become more adept at visual imagery, add a second or even third highlight. You'll find that you can run through two or more scenarios during each session.

Visualize yourself becoming absorbed in this activity without any consideration of the clock. For example, see yourself creatively solving a problem or successfully motivating someone to complete a presentation. Acknowledge that time is not a factor in this image. As you see yourself completing a sale or finalizing year-end numbers, notice how good it feels not to have the pressure of the clock.

3. Clear your mind and relax. Take a few deep breaths, exhaling slowly.

4. Bring the image into focus again. Once more observe the positive sensation of being engrossed in this activity. Feel how natural it seems to be free of the pressure of mechanical time.

5. As you focus on your intentional timeless now, give that image positive energy with an affirmation. See that particular highlight of your day as if it were already happening. Make a strong, affirmative statement about releasing unnecessary scheduling according to the clock by creating intentional timeless moments. Say "Today I allow myself to experience timeless now moments."

Repeat this exercise in the evening, visualizing highlights of the coming day.

Whenever this image of accomplishing your highlight appears throughout the day, acknowledge it. Focus on the experience, but always in a light, gentle way. Don't force the issue; just let it happen. See your now moment occur as you desire it to take place. And always end this spontaneous visual imagery session with an affirmation.

As soon as you feel comfortable with this exercise, add one or more highlights to your visual imagery program both morning and evening. And during the day, gradually allow yourself to accomplish more activities without referring to the clock.

GETTING STUCK

Sometimes, as you sit down to relax and begin to focus on the intentional timeless nows, you'll draw a blank. Nothing happens. You sit there feeling frustrated.

Most likely you're not completely relaxed. Successful visual imagery requires that your mind and body be deeply relaxed for your brain-wave patterns to change and slow down. This deeper, slower level is called the alpha level, and it is in this state that we are more receptive to behavioral changes. If you practice meditation, you're already familiar with the alpha level.

Check your relaxation by taking some slow, deep breaths. Then run through your relaxation exercise again.

If your visual imaging receiver is still not working well, you may be experiencing a creative block. To work through this problem and identify your now moments, follow this clearing exercise.

1. Take a sheet of paper and write at the top "The reason I can't let go of unnecessary scheduling is . . ." Immediately list any thoughts that come into your head to complete the sentence.

2. Sit quietly with your list and read it over. What kind of limitations on the way you view time do these thoughts indicate? Do any of these thoughts "click" for you?

3. Now write a list under the heading "The reasons I can let go of unnecessary scheduling are . . ." If your list starts to flow, you are ready to return to the visualization exercise. If not, repeat the exercise until you have revealed the suppressed problem that is causing you to shut down.

NOW TIME IN ACTION

No doubt you are wondering how practical this intentional timeless-now visualization really is, particularly when you try to follow it up without reference to the clock. Doesn't the world run on clock time? Doesn't it demand mechanical synchronization?

Yes and no.

First of all, keep in mind during this initial week of deceleration, as you visualize the highlights of your day, that your goal isn't to eradicate time cues from your planning style. Rather, you're working toward releasing *unnecessary* scheduling by focusing on intentional timeless nows.

This exercise does assume that you know the difference between essential and nonessential scheduling, and perhaps you aren't really certain of that difference. Don't feel bad if that's the case. The truth is, most of us are afraid to release our hold on time because we're convinced that our schedule is our power source. So we schedule out of fear as often as we do from need. Only as we practice highlighting now moments in our day do we come to see how much pressure we add by scheduling errands or appointments that don't really require it.

So, here you are. You wake up in the morning with the best intentions. You find a quiet place and go through the visual imagery exercise. After showering, you sit down to breakfast. So far, so good. Driving to work, however, you sense your resolve slipping. You begin to wonder how you will maintain the image of your intentional timeless now throughout your day. The idea sounded reasonable while you were in the privacy of your bedroom, but the closer you get to the office and all the hassle that's awaiting you, the more fuzzy the exercise seems.

First, stop intellectualizing. Trust results from commitment. Resist the urge to overanalyze the exercise. You've identified an intentional timeless now to experience today. Give your subconscious some credit. It's a powerful energy source if only you allow it to work for you.

Do, however, simplify the job. For this first week, highlight experiences without an obvious time tag. Choose a high point or points in your day over which you have control of the time element. For example, visual imagery may show you preparing a month-end inventory report and having an appointment with your boss to discuss a raise. You'd be wise to visualize yourself working on that report rather than focusing on the more crucial meeting with your boss. And remember, this exercise is only a starting point. As it becomes more natural for you to build intentional timeless nows into your day, you'll gradually exercise more control over your time, even more than you'd expected.

Put everything you've got to work for you. Support your subconscious by making your conscious mind aware of your intent. When both are involved, one level of consciousness reinforces the other.

As you begin to use visual imagery to focus on the highlights of your day, here are fourteen ideas to support you if you get off track. Any one can serve as a reminder to nudge you back to the now.

1. Choose a habitual experience and treat it as a timeless moment. For example, you may select your morning shower. As you stand under the spray, sense the surge of the pulsating stream as it strikes your body. Notice how the water feels as it comes in contact with your face, your neck, your arms, and your hands. Concentrate on the sound the water makes as it splashes on your skin and on the tile. Experience the slippery-smooth surface of the soap. Inhale the spicy fragrance of the shampoo. Focus all your senses on this simple, routine task. If your mind begins to wander, notice why it moves from the now moment. Is it because you are entertaining a past thought or projecting into the future? Deliberately refocus your attention on the present.

Compare the intensity of that experience with the way you usually shower. Notice how different it felt to be completely focused on one task.

2. Decide not to wear your watch for a certain part of the day. Physically removing time is an excellent way to remind yourself that you are working on creating intentional timeless nows. If you're uncomfortable without a watch during the workweek, go without it on Saturday or Sunday of the following weekend. Notice how you function that day without your familiar timepiece. If this makes you feel surer of yourself, remove your wristwatch on a workday the next week when your schedule seems relatively undemanding. You'll be surprised to find that you naturally set your own comfortable pace.

3. For three days this week, set your alarm at varying earlier times than usual. Six o'clock or even six-thirty *feels* different from a habitual seven-fifteen. Each morning when you wake up, listen to the new morning sounds. Pay attention to how the light comes into the room. Let the reality of this moment register completely on your experience. Giving yourself totally to this slightly different intentional now gently reinforces your commitment to create intentional timeless moments throughout your day.

4. When you are stopped at a traffic light on a morning drive or waiting for a train or bus, use the moment to focus on the highlight you are going to experience today. Notice how you feel when you see yourself engrossed in that activity. Hold that image and repeat your affirmation, "Today I allow myself to enjoy intentional timeless nows." Or create your own affirmation that relates directly to that image.

5. Whenever you feel overwhelmed, you may find that visualizing a tightly covered pot of boiling water will help you refocus. See the pressure building inside the pot. Transfer that image to the way you see your day and schedule. Now imagine that you are removing the lid from the pot. Allow the steam to release into the air. Watch it rise and disappear. Experience a sense of relief, release, and rest as the steam escapes. Letting go of the past and the future (everything, that is, except the steam escaping now) frees you to immerse yourself in the present.

6. At work, switch the sequence of some of your more routine tasks. Try reading your mail—or at least your less urgent stack of mail—in the afternoon instead of in the morning. Trade with a friend so you can take a coffee break at eleven o'clock instead of at ten. Because habit is a great duller of immediate experience, doing a routine task in a new way or at a different time can infuse you with a fresh perspective.

And a new viewpoint reinforces your goal of living with intentional timeless nows.

7. Change your work scene if possible. Rearrange your furniture or have a lunch meeting catered in instead of scheduled at your regular restaurant. Physical changes give visual cues that remind you of your intention. Changing the scene literally alters your view, which affects how you construe experiences.

8. Build flexibility into your routine by planning an open-ended meeting for one day late in the week. If your work environment is conducive—few enough people working in close proximity—plan a meeting casually for "sometime in the morning." After you've met, consider how you felt about meeting without a schedule.

You may be surprised how little resistance you'll encounter when you suggest this idea. While it would have sounded radical in the 1970s and even, to some extent, in the 1980s, today business and industry are rapidly moving in a direction that supports individualism. Companies are recognizing that self-motivated people are the most productive employees. With this realization has come a more relaxed attitude toward scheduled time.

For instance, at one of the plant operations of W. L. Gore, part of a worldwide electronics firm that manufactures GORE-TEX and high-reliability wire and cable products, meetings are rarely scheduled. Associate David McCarter explains, "Our company does have an unusual attitude about time. The whole company is task oriented. We have almost nothing routinely scheduled. We do schedule planning meetings but the dates are loose. We run on regular hours because our customers depend on it. But we go longer rather than shorter. We are service oriented. With 130 employees in this office, we stagger people's hours because we want to provide the best service. Some concentrate on East Coast customers and come in to work earlier, two or three hours earlier."

9. Make one day a flex-day. Don't schedule anything.

Commit to no appointments. Put away your pocket calendar and even your to-do list. For this one day, don't synchronize your calendar with anyone. Act only on your timeless intentional nows and respond to the moment. If you decide to try this early in your deceleration program, you may feel more comfortable designating a weekend day as your first flex-day. Or you don't need to make it an entire day. You can try it at first just for a morning or an afternoon.

One executive who practices this frequently is Doug Greene, the thirty-nine-year-old president of New Hope Communications. Greene's business is a $5 million company originally based in New Hope, Pennsylvania, that markets health foods and publishes two magazines.

"I call my no-appointment days 'Doug days,'" Green says, adding that he gets his best ideas when doing whatever he pleases, whether that involves going to a museum or taking a long walk. "Doug Days," which physically and mentally remove him from his usual routine, recharge his creative powers.

At home ...

10. Take up a new sport or hobby. Confronted with a physical challenge of mastering a stem christie turn or moving through the gears of a powerful sports car, who can think of anything else? Learning to do something new refocuses your attention and releases it from the clock. One note of caution, however. If you decide to follow up on this suggestion, be sure to select an activity or sport that doesn't depend on the clock to determine success or achievement.

11. Create an intentionally timeless experience out of an errand by changing your routine. Bicycle instead of drive to a friend's home; it will change how you perceive the scenery. Or explore a different route when you go the grocery. By altering your routine, you open yourself to new and unexpected experiences, each one of which has the potential for becoming a timeless now. We often do this for ourselves during vacations, but why limit such a renewing experience to just a few times a year?

12. Treat yourself to a sauna or Jacuzzi and use these soothing sessions to focus on intentional timelessness. Steam or water makes an ideal environment in which to practice visual imagery. After you have focused on the highlights of your day, take a mental inventory of all the positive reinforcement you've received that day that supports your goal of intentional nows.

13. Change the time and place of your mealtimes. Eat dinner later than usual. Have lunch or breakfast on the patio. Prepare different dishes using ingredients you don't normally buy. Mealtimes offer unlimited opportunities to engage all your senses while renewing a habitual experience.

14. Make your vacation an intentional timeless week. Decide to live for the entire period without a schedule. Larry Wilson, best-selling author, founder of Wilson Learning, and CEO of LEAP—Leaders' Experiential Adventure Program—based in Santa Fe, New Mexico, devotes his energies to helping Fortune 500 executives and their employees become better learners. Wilson, who uses visualization daily, admits to living on the fast track. So he commits to spending one week out of every six on an island, using this time as a physical, mental, and spiritual retreat. "I set this week aside as rejuvenation time," says Wilson. "I go to the Cayman Islands. I seem to get clarity there. I reenergize. That's where I get my best ideas."

A single parent of two elementary-age children experimented successfully with intentional timelessness over a summer vacation. For three months the family decided not to set alarms. Everybody woke up whenever they felt like it. They ate when they were hungry. They ignored the clock. No activities were planned. Instead, they did things together or separately as they felt like it. If they got up in the morning and decided to drive two hours to a beautiful resort town, that's what they did that day. At the end of the three months, the mother concluded that the summer experiment had upgraded everyone's quality of life. The children reestablished their biological rhythms. Everyone seemed to eat more nutritious foods and sleep better, and they grew closer as a family. Setting their own pace gave this family a sense of grace that had been missing in their hectic, clock-driven lifestyle.

If you can't take three months away from the clock, try this family's experiment on a weekend or a holiday. Interrupting the clock routine can put everyone in a household in touch with now.

NEW TIME RESULTS

If you still need convincing, here is more testimony from successful people who are living with intentional now moments. If they can do it, why not you?

"Because I am very intuitive, I don't allocate time. I just give it whatever it needs," says Michael Russell of American City Business Journals. After beginning his day with visualization, Russell lives deliberately in the present. "I live with a real sense of urgency, but I don't put additional burdens on myself by scheduling. A lot of things I simply don't schedule. For instance, I try not to schedule meetings. Very seldom will anyone have a set meeting with me at eleven o'clock. I'm much more likely to pick up the phone and get my business done that way. Then, too, if I am in the midst of an appointment and finish, I quit early. By the same token, I'll reschedule an extra hour if I need it, if the meeting is worthy of that extra hour."

A CEO of a Western-based $20 million company confides, "I had to make a conscious decision to make the change to creating intentional timeless nows. To my advantage, I had such a strong desire to eliminate the feelings of stress, to clear up mind clutter, that my passion for change allowed me to adjust more easily. To do this, however, I had to accept the responsibility that I had the power to create my situation just as I had accepted the fact that I had the power to stop drinking. It was the realization of my power and relentless desire for joy in my life that led me to find ways to live more in the moment. At first, as each situation occurred in my day, I would consciously fixate on what I was doing at that moment. But eventually I trained myself to eliminate superfluous thoughts. This takes tremendous concentration. But if you truly desire to live in the now, you can."

Says a forty-two-year-old telecommunications business executive: "Frankly, at first it was difficult for me to even begin to think of focusing on the now. For a while, it created more stress for me trying to make the change than living without it. But then I realized that what was wrong was that I did not have 100 percent intent to make this change. I was intellectualizing too much about it. Finally, for two weeks I gave 100 percent to making the change of incorporating intentional timeless moments into my day. I did this by listening to my heart all day long rather than my head. And I found that each day got easier for me because I was feeling happier in the process. Events that previously would have 'set me off' didn't have much negative effect because I was releasing stress and I was relaxing focusing on these highlights. I kept the same schedule, but my perception changed about the events I was doing. I started taking myself less seriously and started laughing more about some of the crazy things I created in my daily life. Now when I get out of focus, I listen with my heart and let go of what my head is telling me."

A thirty-six-year-old investment broker with a major Wall Street firm recalls: "The concept of living in the now sounded idealistic to me until I consciously thought about it, and it became clear that my life is all a now moment and will always be a now moment. So two years ago I decided why not live it that way intentionally?"

"What's wonderful about a group experience of being in the timeless now is that the action becomes the reward," says futurist Barbara Marx Hubbard. Describing the group meditation experience she participates in regularly, Hubbard discloses, "It feels so good to do this—to connect at the core of your being—that you do it because it feels good, instead of because you have to do it. I always feel an immense relaxation during this exercise."

"I was originally in practice as an oral surgeon," says Jerry Burnette, a dentist recounting his journey to the now. "My practice was growing and I was considered successful by traditional medical standards, but I became increasingly frustrated with my life. I decided I had to find out who I was. I left dentistry and moved out of the country and explored several different avenues. What I came to after a number of years was a realization of how important it was for me to let go intellectually and spiritually—and not take back what I released. It was during this period that I began to understand the concept of intentional timeless nows and how important these are for my well-being.

"Subsequently, I made the decision to come back to dentistry. But I now approach my whole life in a completely different way. One way I create intentional now moments is through listening to and participating in jazz. Music is a medium that lets me transcend time. I also use the Jacuzzi and steam for this purpose. There I consciously disconnect from the people around me and immerse myself in intentional nows. I've found that specific visualization or meditation techniques don't work as well for me as incorporating my intentional nows as part of other activities I enjoy during the day."

PAUSE FOR REFLECTION

At the end of week one you have discovered three important facts about time.

1. Creating intentional now moments makes you aware of overscheduling and unnecessary clock-induced pressure.
2. In experiencing intentional nows, you see how pleasurable it is to live with timelessness.
3. Trusting in intentional timelessness gives you courage to release the clock.

6

Week Two:
Going Within for Balance

THE MESSAGE OF THE TAO:
Holding to the Center

To hold to the center is to listen to the voice of inner mind.
To follow one is to be in harmony with the other.

We've been living with a false concept of balance. Traditional time management has taught us that we can achieve balance by dividing our time into neat compartments (labeled "social," "emotional," "physical," "mental," even "spiritual") and carefully monitoring the hours and effort given to each. According to traditional theory, balance results when we manage our time so that no compartment is ignored. In fact, this practice promotes an artificial equilibrium, a constantly moving point of parity that is overly dependent on outside time demands. Because this concept of compartmentalized time binds us tighter to the clock, it inhibits us from moving at our own pace.

Natural balance is not a product of outside cues. It resides within each of us. It is as instinctive as breathing, as innate as our pulse rates. We reveal our natural balance when we are aligned with our individual pace and rhythms. Whenever we act more from our personal point of balance and respond less to outside cues, we gradually and naturally release the pressure of the clock.

Key Time Phrase:
Respond to inner rhythms rather than react to the clock.

Key Time Issue:
In discovering our natural balance, clock time diminishes in importance.

Inner Time Result:
Participation in activities becomes a function of knowing our balance and rhythms and choosing a pace that is aligned with each.

Inner Time Technique:
Using natural rhythms to guide our actions.

Balancing from within is that serendipitous experience in which we are at ease with ourselves and our commitments. All of us have encountered this exquisite feeling at least occasionally, knowing that, for this moment, all is truly right with our world. We know when we are in balance because we get some very strong signals. We feel good, not anxious or pressured. We feel joy. We're at peace. Most of all, *we feel comfortable with the tempo of our lives.*

This state of balance is not mysterious. It's the way we would choose to be if we had the choice. That we all, in fact, do have this choice becomes clear as one begins deceleration.

Unhappily, most of us ignore our inner signals. We approach life as if it were a teeter-totter. We work hard and play hard, continuously careening from highs to lows—from boredom to excitement, peacefulness to panic, euphoria to depression. We load our schedules with commitments in the mistaken belief that if only we can do enough different things in a day, we'll feel more balanced.

Believing that the best balance is achieved when we handle all kinds of social time demands adroitly sets us up for failure. Convinced that we must have time and energy not only for our jobs, our families, and ourselves but also for other worthwhile relationships and commitments, we put ourselves in a no-win situation. No wonder we feel pressure. During difficult times, confined by agendas we don't control or constrained to work by others' clocks, we console ourselves that this is the price we pay for living in a communal society. And to a large degree, it is.

However, we can learn to control these pressures. Holding to the center—openly acknowledging and continually adjusting our natural equilibrium—lets us balance our personal needs with our perceived responsibilities. Balance results when we equalize internal and external pressures.

ESTABLISHING BALANCE

For the second week of this program you'll be concentrating on two concepts. First, you will focus on your natural state of balance so that you can evaluate how the decisions you make concerning time affect you physically and emotionally. Second, you'll become aware of your body rhythms so that you work *with* these fluctuations in mood, energy, and skill level as you plan your day. When you put these two together—balance and sensitivity to your rhythms—you create your own planning tool.

The brief visualization exercise for this week is designed to help you identify your point of balance. Use the same periods in the morning and evening that you set aside last week to work on intentional now moments, picking a place where you won't be interrupted and where you are settled in the same comfortable manner.

Again you start by relaxing, but in a different way. The relaxation exercise for balance visualization is circular deep breathing. This is a centuries-old technique used successfully in yoga and is quite easy.

Begin by inhaling slowly, deeply, and completely. Exhale slowly. Immediately complete the circle by taking in a second deep breath. Follow this with a rhythmical deep exhalation. Continue breathing rhythmically and deeply without interruption.

Within minutes of beginning circular deep breathing you will begin to feel relaxed and peaceful. As you continue breathing, notice that time, as we usually mark it, appears suspended. Notice, too, that you are now acutely aware of your inner currents. Focusing on breathing in this manner enables you to observe the natural ebb and flow of your physical system. As you continue to breathe rhythmically, you naturally align yourself with these inner rhythms.

When you feel completely relaxed, you are ready to begin to visualize balance.

1. With your eyes closed, see yourself floating in a body of water—a pool or lake. Position yourself on an inflatable raft or air mattress, or (if you float comfortably in the water) imagine yourself drifting effortlessly on your back. When you have this image in your mind, enjoy the buoyant sensation of the water as it gently supports you. Feel the water gently rock you from side to side. Immerse yourself in weightlessness. Think about how effortless it feels to float on the surface of the pool or lake. Focus on the easy, soothing motion of the water and give yourself over to the sensation of being totally, physically balanced. Again, remember that all people experience different sensations as they visualize. Whatever you "see," accept it. Hold that image. Now release it and bring it up again.

2. Release that scene. Once more erase your mental slate.

3. Relaxed, picture a particular day or a time when you felt supremely confident about your life. Allow this image to float freely to the surface of your consciousness. Maybe you recall a project you had put together that was an overwhelming success. It had been a challenge, but had also been a lot of fun. As you worked on it, everything seemed to fall into place. You remember feeling a sense of exquisite relief, of joy and peace when all that good work came to fruition. Nothing seemed difficult. Everything seemed easy.

Or perhaps you remember a family vacation when you retired to a cabin after a busy day sightseeing. You see yourself, your spouse, and children all sitting together around the table playing cards. The family is peaceful, relaxed, and happy. At this moment, you know that all is right with your world.

Whatever image you select, see it in detail. If it's easier for you to sense rather than picture the image, re-create the feelings it engendered.

4. Let your mind rove over this image, taking in all the detail and experiencing all the sensations.

5. Imagine yourself feeling this sense of exquisite balance all the time. Imagine it as a *perpetual* experience. What you are feeling is the sensation of being completely aligned with your inner and outer environments.

6. Affirm this image with this statement: "I let go of striving to make things happen and allow events to take place according to my pace."

Repeat this exercise in the evening.

During this week of deceleration, before you agree to any *significant* time commitment, measure it against this image of natural balance. Significant time decisions consume time and/or energy. They are the items you'd star or underline if you saw them on a to-do list; they would qualify as As or Bs under traditional time management standards. Often they involve a commitment that goes beyond a single day's activity.

Before deciding whether or not to take action on that significant time request, recall the image of natural balance that you created. For a moment immerse yourself in that balanced state. Now picture yourself involved in the activity you are considering.

Ask yourself: What will that activity require in terms of responsibilities? What can I gain from it? What do I stand to lose? What's the time frame involved? Does it feel comfortable to me? Is it rushed?

As you think about that opportunity, compare your emotional response with how you feel when you are in balance. If you sense peace, joy, excitement, ease—or simply that this could be fun to do—you know that it won't upset your natural equilibrium.

On the other hand, if thinking about it this way makes you feel anxious, agitated, or tense, acknowledge that as well, and if possible don't commit to that obligation this week. As you progress with deceleration, you'll find that often you can reconfigure the appointment or event so that it better suits your natural pace and rhythms. But for this week, to borrow a phrase from Buckminster Fuller. "If in doubt, don't."

Of course you probably already have some time commitments in place that you aren't entirely comfortable with. Maybe you have a rush project you wish you hadn't accepted or are involved in a committee that is taking up more time than you anticipated. Live with them. Don't attempt to undo those obligations. The object of this exercise isn't to create more chaos in your life, it's to help you make your days run smoother from now on.

For week two of deceleration, confine your balance checks to significant *new* activities you are considering taking on. The time to consider how an appointment, project, or event will affect your natural balance is *before* you agree to it—not afterward.

GETTING STUCK

Because balance is such a delicate state of mind, outside influences will occasionally interfere with successful visualization. If this should happen to you, don't try to force an image. Instead, sit quietly and take a few deep, circular breaths. Try to unblock through relaxing.

If you still have difficulty creating an image of balance, try this clearing technique.

1. Sitting quietly, try to sense what you are feeling in your body. Are you feeling discomfort anywhere? A headache? Stomach pain? Clenched jaw? Notice any tense or uncomfortable areas. Consider, too, whether you're experiencing something less concrete, such as an inability to focus your thoughts. Center your attention on your area of discomfort.

2. Close your eyes and recall the image of you floating on water. Let that peaceful sensation surround you. Allow the soothing water to cleanse the affected area. Relax as the tension seeps out of your body. Take a few deep breaths and hold that peaceful image.

3. Now open your eyes, take a sheet of paper, and write, "The reasons I cannot remain comfortably balanced are . . ." As you review the list, notice how your body responds as you read through your answers. Do you sense tension anywhere? Do you get an uncomfortable feeling?

4. Make a second heading: "The reasons I can stay comfortably balanced are . . ." and write that list. As you read what you have written, pay attention to what your body is telling you. Do you feel relaxed and at ease? Physical relaxation is a clue to inner peace. Once you've achieved this peaceful state, you're ready to return to the visualization exercise. If you still don't feel entirely comfortable, repeat the clearing technique until you have uncovered the reason for your mental block.

TIME, BALANCE, AND RHYTHMS

A funny thing happens as you become aware of your natural balance. You notice that you lose it a lot.

What's going on?

We all know that flux is our natural condition. Each of us reacts to hundreds of inner clocks that operate on hourly, daily, weekly, monthly, even yearly cycles. This complex system of timekeepers, as profound as our hearts and as obvious as fingernails, regulates everything about us from our body temperature to behavioral reactions. Research shows that biological clocks influence our moods, our ability to handle stress, and even the times when we are most susceptible to accidents and illness.

Not surprisingly, these internal pacemakers can and do sway our equilibrium, which is why we need to be aware of how our rhythms affect balance and how balance in turn affects time.

Rhythms and Balance

Chronobiology, the study of these biological body clocks, is a relatively new scientific discipline. Living clocks were first explored by French astronomer Jean de Mairan, who in 1729 expressed curiosity as to why the heliotrope plant opened its leaves to light and closed them to dusk independent of the amount of sunlight falling on it. It wasn't until the mid-1950s, however, that a Stanford University professor, Colin Pittendrigh, proved that clocks exist in life-forms as simple as a single-celled organism and as complex as man. Pittendrigh's research led him to conclude that biological clocks are a fundamental property of life and that these internal clocks are affected by external timekeepers almost as if two oscillators are operating simultaneously, one inside and one outside the body.

These biological rhythms—what may more accurately be described as orderly fluctuations—cycle continually. Although sequences aren't absolute—women who live together, for instance, often establish similar menstrual cycles—our rhythms are as distinctive as our fingerprints. And like our fingerprints, our biological rhythms touch everything we touch in our day. They influence when we wake, how we sleep, what we eat, when we love, and how effectively we work and play.

Much has been made of the distinction between morning and night people, the so-called larks and owls. This is a fairly obvious rhythmic variation, one that's easy to observe. If you stumble around in the morning until ten or eleven and come to life when the sun goes down, you fit the owl profile. On the other hand, if you wake up early, eager to run two miles, and then come in smiling and talkative at breakfast, you're a definite lark. Owls are wise not to schedule important meetings at breakfast, while larks are smart to pack more critical appointments into the morning and afternoon hours, leaving evenings for relaxation.

While this explanation may sound simplistic, it's quite accurate. Most of us instinctively know where we perch. We may not know, however, that morning people are better off to follow a regular daily routine since larks more than owls tend to have greater difficulty adjusting to changes that affect body rhythms.

But there's more to body rhythms than being a day or night person. In addition to circadian rhythms—the sleep/wake cycle—we react to weekly, monthly, seasonal, even annual rhythmic beats. And we also keep pace with myriad subtle physical changes like shifts in body temperature, blood pressure, hormonal excretion, and cell division.

Given the quantity and sensitivity of all these inner clocks, it's no wonder that occasionally we get out of sync. When we have a late night, travel across time zones, or change our work shift from days to evenings, we usually know it. We feel dull and sluggish and drag around until our body clock slowly readjusts. These kinds of dramatic changes are so obvious that we are forced to accommodate them. Happily, given time, we naturally recycle and get back on our familiar track.

But what about those more subtle signals that affect how we go through our day? We get a sudden surge of energy at

4:30 P.M. and schedule a racquetball game for 6:00. After lunch, we experience a wave of tiredness and are late for an appointment. While giving a presentation in the late afternoon, we inexplicably forget the name of a supplier. And, although we ate a big dinner, an hour and a half later we're rummaging in the refrigerator.

What's going on? Rhythms! Each instance is a clear sign that our cycles are operating and we should be paying attention to them. But which of us does? What usually happens is that we're so intent on covering an agenda or completing an activity in the time we've set for ourselves, we disregard these body bulletins. We plunge ahead on automatic and wonder, later, why the racquetball game took forever to complete, why the presentation seemed so difficult to make, or why we ate that leftover piece of rhubarb pie.

Rhythms are real and predictable. Once you learn how to read them, you can use these inner signals to guide you as you organize your day.

An excellent book on this subject is *The Secrets Our Body Clocks Reveal* by Susan Perry and Jim Dawson. In it the authors draw a general profile of rhythms and body cycles. Although each of us is a highly individual organism and no two clocks on any two people are ever set exactly alike, some behaviors, Perry and Dawson explain, are basic. Knowing the norm, you can draw your own profile. Here are some pertinent facts on rhythms and cycles culled from facts that Perry and Dawson compiled.

• Alertness levels. Generally we peak at noon, but most of us experience a severe dip in energy and concentration soon afterward that can last up to a couple of hours. Alertness levels start to rise again in midafternoon. We are least alert in the early morning, between 3:00 A.M. and 6:00 A.M.

• Memory. Short-term memory is best in the morning— about 15 percent more efficient than at any other time of the day. Long-term memory, however, is strongest during the afternoon.

• Thinking. Mornings, particularly late mornings, are best for cognitive tasks. That's the time for those creative or complex assignments requiring reasoning or organizational skills.

• "Mindless" activities. Do uncomplicated jobs, such as washing the car or photocopying, in the midafternoon. This is the time for jobs that require no memory or thinking skills.

• Manual dexterity. Hand-eye coordination peaks in the afternoon, which makes this time of day ideal for typing, carpentry projects, or such activities as practicing an instrument.

• Moods. Although a wide variety of influences cause our moods to fluctuate, chronobiology indicates that we generally reach our happiness peak about four hours after we wake up. Late morning, then, is our most "up" time of day. It's when we're more apt to feel that we can do those projects that stumped us the morning or night before.

• Sensory clues. All our senses—taste, touch, hearing, sight, and smell—are most acute during the twilight hours of early evening. Perry and Dawson suggest that this is why dinner tastes better to us than breakfast, why bright lights are irritating at night, and children seem noisier when we come home from work than in the morning!

• Judging time. Our perception of time is tied to our body temperature. Time flies faster for us when our body temperature is low in the early morning and late evening. When our body temperature rises, in the afternoon and into early evening, our sense of time slows down. This is why when we're ill with a fever, time seems to grind to a halt.

• Physical prowess. Late afternoon and early evening are our peak physical time. It's when we're most coordinated, when we are able to react quickest to outside stimuli. Studies have shown that we perceive a physical workout to be easier and less tiring in late afternoon. Perry and Dawson conclude that we're most likely to work harder and get more out of a late-afternoon or early-evening workout than a morning or early-afternoon one.

In addition to living with all these rhythms, we also respond to various cycles. Many body functions are set to ninety-minute cycles. We daydream, feel sleepy, urinate, and get an urge to snack or to smoke or chew gum or just put something other than food in our mouths about every hour and a half. Stress or boredom can shorten this cycle to every sixty minutes.

For this week, instead of doing things strictly by the clock, try to organize according to your rhythmic signals. Using your rhythms as your planning guide, shift your focus from outside cues to inner needs. You'll find, as you adjust your routine to better suit your natural tempo, that work becomes more pleasurable. Tasks are easier when you do them at your own pace and accomplish them when you're at your best. Not only do you see your best results, you reap the most satisfaction. If you always run in the morning, try running after work before dinner this week to test your rhythms. If you are planning a lengthy meeting that usually goes two hours before a break, this week break after an hour and a half and see how everyone responds. If you're most alert in the mornings yet always fill them with scheduled meetings, try shifting some of those sessions to the afternoon to give yourself a block of high-energy, productive time.

When planning from balance, consider the full range of cycles.

• Seasons of life. As you think about your schedule this week, consider the time of year. Most people respond to the seasons. Personalities tend to flower in the summer and turn inward in the winter. Consider when you are at your best. If this is a "down" season for you, be aware of it. Maybe you can put off starting that big project until you've reached a better place in the calendar. At the very least, be kind to yourself if this isn't your best time of year.

• Time of the month. Women are very sensitive to monthly cycles, but men have cycles, too. Male hormones fluctuate, weight changes, and even beard growth shows a rhythm every thirty days. Your physical and emotional state can fluctuate with the phases of the moon. Emergency room physicians, for instance, know that a full moon brings out the most bizarre behavior in both sexes. And even women who don't suffer from premenstrual syndrome usually experience a mild depression before the onset of their menstrual cycle. If you are sensitive to monthly cyclical behaviors, taking a "reading" on your time of the month can help you gauge your energy and your tolerance level.

• Time of day. Although even an extreme owl is set only about two hours ahead of an average lark, these differences can be felt keenly. Whenever possible this week, fine-tune your schedule to suit your time frame. Sometimes small changes can make a big difference. Larks could plan to interrupt an unavoidable late-night work session with lots of exercise breaks to keep them alert, while reluctant owls should allow themselves plenty of extra time to wake up before heading out for an 8:00 A.M. exam.

• Factor in your sleep quotient. Be honest about how much sleep you require. Do you have difficulty sleeping in a different time zone? How do you react when your sleep pattern changes? Although we require less sleep as we grow older, as we age we also become less flexible in our ability to handle time changes. When planning evening activities this week, be sensitive to your sleep requirement and don't fight it.

• Anticipate your sexual desires. Sexual drive peaks in the early morning. If you're too tired for romantic evenings and too pressed or separated for "nooners," relax. This week, set your alarm earlier and enjoy that extra time in bed.

Beyond cyclical factors, there are other considerations to think about as you plan your activities this week, many of them related to previously cited Perry and Dawson norms.

• When is your thinking at its best? If you have a presentation to make or a creative session to run, can you schedule it during your peak time when your cognitive skills are sharpest?

• What about your moods? As you make appointments and plan work sessions, acknowledge your "down" times, those predictable periods when your mood and physical energies sag. For this week avoid scheduling intense activities during those periods.

• Anticipate stress. Avoid stressful situations that will intensify negative feedback. Instead of working up to the moment of a deadline, for instance, give yourself a day's "fudge factor" to ease the tension. If you have to face a stressful situation this week, allow yourself extra time that day to attend to your more frequent cyclical needs to eat, sleep, and so on. If the situation entails extensive writing or computational work, plan on taking a walk or getting up from your desk every ninety minutes or so.

• Expect an early-afternoon energy dip. If you've got an important appointment scheduled for that after-lunch slump, have lunch later than usual so that you feed that slump with high-energy food. For instance, if you have an important two o'clock meeting, eat at one instead of noon, or even twelve-thirty. If nothing's pressing, give in to that sleepy urge and take a "power nap." Regular nappers insist that even fifteen minutes refreshes them and charges their energy.

• Treat yourself to a daily dose of sunlight. Because we are biological creatures, getting at least fifteen minutes of natural sunlight every day helps our rhythms stay in sync. This week plan to take a fifteen-minute walk at lunchtime to catch some rays. To make up for cloudy middays, and should your office situation permit, position your desk near a window. Or inquire about getting a full-spectrum light that simulates natural sunlight.

Living in Balance

Meet Larry, a businessman who has learned to use his rhythms to guide his daily routine.

Larry, forty-three, is an owl married to Ellen, a lark. A division manager for a medium-size company, he's had to function in a lark-driven world. He has twenty people reporting to him. Because he must meet with these salespeople before they go out on calls each day, his job requires many morning meetings. Mornings, you understand, aren't his peak time. In the afternoon, when he's at his best and could be most productive, Larry's on the road with his senior people making marketing and sales calls.

If he had the choice, he'd turn his mornings and afternoons around. But he doesn't have that option. Consequently, before Larry found his own balance there were times when he felt beleaguered; often he thought he'd never catch up. Worse yet, he didn't see that he had much latitude to change his situation.

When Larry became sensitive to his rhythms and comfortable operating from his point of balance, he realized that he did have options.

He couldn't eliminate those morning meetings without causing problems for twenty people, so he decided to confine that morning meeting to a strategy session. Instead of getting into one-on-one discussions with his staff, he now keeps that meeting general and brief. This frees up morning time for Larry to use to write simple reports, catch up on correspondence, and do other less creative tasks.

Larry now makes travel time do double duty. During stops along the road, he makes afternoon business calls on his car phone for one-on-one sessions with his people. He's at his best in the afternoon, and the car is a less threatening environment than the office, which makes conversation easier.

On very busy days, Larry orders lunch in. He knows that this is a natural high-energy point for him so he takes advantage of it. But he gives himself breathing space after lunch. Instead of packing his schedule with back-to-back appointments starting at 1:00 P.M., he doesn't start appointments until 2:00 P.M., which allows him some time to unwind. On pleasant days he's out for a stroll; on others he catches up on his magazine reading.

Evenings are peak periods for Larry. He used to drag himself out the door to speed-walk with Ellen in the morning. Now he plays racquetball three nights a week. He often takes home heavy business reading to go over after dinner since he's "up" in the evening.

Although Larry used to dread travel, today he's more relaxed. If he has an early-morning meeting in another city, he always tries to take a plane out the night before. If that's not possible, when he boards that 6:00 A.M. flight, he does deep breathing to reduce consciously the stress of getting up earlier than he's accustomed to.

Because he knows that he's not at his best in the morning, Larry carries a pocket tape recorder with him to record sessions. The tape acts as a backup for his memory. Anticipating long sessions without a break, he packs high-energy snacks to get him through hunger attacks. Since breakfast isn't his power period, Larry uses only lunch and dinner for business entertainment.

Sometimes, as you regain your balance, you're surprised by what you find. When Debby Johnson, senior vice president and director of marketing for a national advertising firm based in Oklahoma City, began to pay attention to her natural balance and inner rhythms, she discovered a lot about herself. After she got sick with a prolonged, mysterious illness, she had assumed that the roller-coaster pace of her job was stressing her beyond healthy limits. But it turned out that her pace at work wasn't the problem.

"I found out that the rhythm of my business suits me," she says. "I realized that I'm not somebody who likes long stretches of calm. I thrive on a packed schedule and changes of routine. The pace of this business works for me because even during my most crazed periods, I know that I will always have a couple of quiet days to catch my breath and regroup. While I need those quiet times and enjoy the first day thoroughly, and make it through the second one fine, by day three I can feel myself getting anxious to get moving again. Inevitably, on the third day, something pops!"

Instead of feeling that she had to control her job, Debby adjusted her home routine to balance her unpredictable workday. She wakes up earlier—before her three children—so she has some quiet time to read and think. She anticipates "down" times and doesn't try always to be Superwoman. She even occasionally watches a TV program on a Saturday afternoon and relaxes without guilt. Because she craves regular exercise, Debby considers her ballet class a priority. She also makes certain that she gets enough sleep. These subtle changes keep her moving at a comfortable pace.

Just as Larry and Debby learned to use their rhythms to find their natural balance, you can, too.

Quick Balance Checks

No matter how effectively you concentrate on balance this week, there will be times when you get out of sync. Snags can send you reeling. Unexpected surprises can throw you off. To help you get back on center, use either of these quick checks.

• Visualize a dial with numbers ranging from 1 to 10. A 5 indicates where you feel most at ease. Imagine the dial moving toward that number. It may bounce around for a few seconds. But gradually it registers 5. Take a few deep breaths in and out while you hold that image. Repeat the affirmation: "I let go of striving to make things happen and allow events to take place according to my pace."

• Choose a symbol that represents your image of balance.

If you're not acrophobic, picture yourself on a high-wire high above the earth. If you prefer to stay closer to the ground, you might see yourself learning to ride a bicycle, experiencing that amazing moment when you stop wobbling from side to side and head down the sidewalk under your own power. If you prefer a more metaphysical image, see yourself in the middle of a pyramid—an ancient symbol of energy in perfect balance. Feel yourself gathering and refocusing your energies as you see the symbol. Breathe in and out rhythmically. Repeat the affirmation: "I let go of striving to make things happen and allow events to take place according to my pace."

Now that you are putting balance and rhythms together, you're ready to let time fly.

The Fun Factor

A paperweight embossed with these words sits on employees' desks throughout Levi Strauss & Co.: "We want satisfaction from accomplishments and friendships, balanced personal and professional lives, and to have fun in our endeavors."

The fun factor is the best and easiest way to monitor your equilibrium because if an activity sounds as if it will be "fun" to do, you can be sure that it suits your natural balance and rhythms. But what, exactly, is this thing called "fun"?

"Fun is when you are doing the things that are right for you all the time," offers Doug Greene of New Hope Communications. "Fun isn't all laughter. It can be serious business."

"To me, fun isn't anything extra," says Jim Lea, a Park City, Utah, realtor, avid skier, and cyclist. "I've always operated in the mode of fun. It's necessary to my sense of balance."

"Fun isn't frivolous," agrees Debby Johnson. "It makes good sense. I always tell my associates, 'Don't take on this project unless you think it's fun.' Amazingly, fun is something that most of them would not even consider."

Fun can be the sense of enjoyment when you're doing something, a sense of accomplishment when you're finished, and the feeling, when you look back on what you did, that you're glad you did it. Sometimes it registers as a quiet sense of satisfaction. Other times it's felt as relaxation. It can be as mild as "interest" or as strong as "rapture."

Fun is an indicator and not an insulator of your emotions, so there are no guarantees that you'll continue having fun as you get into a project. You may think it will be pleasurable as you consider it, only to have it turn into a bear. Still, at the very least, fun is a good measure of how you feel about an activity at the onset.

Everyone knows that time flies when you're having fun. But do you know why? Apart from the physical factors that link body temperature to our perception of time, emotional factors contribute to the aerodynamics of fun. When you're having fun, you're completely absorbed in what you're doing. Time becomes meaningless. You experience a timeless now. Because you don't pay any attention to the clock, the minutes and hours pass without your knowing it. You look up to find time has "flown."

On another level, when you appreciate an activity as fun, you charge it with positive energy. This energy becomes an emotional jet stream that literally carries you along, a high that also helps time "fly."

For this second week of deceleration, let the fun factor be your guide whenever you consider a significant New Time commitment. After measuring this activity against your image of natural balance, check yourself by asking "Will this be fun for me to do?" Listen to your inner mind and respect the answer.

"This is the gauge on your dashboard that you should watch," says Doug Greene. "To me, the important measure is are you having any fun!"

Sometimes you will get conflicting messages. Your logical self tells you to go for it, but your intuitive side sends up red flags. What do you do?

Greene confides that when this happens to him, he keeps processing the decision. "I ask: What else must I add to this? Where am I blocked? What do I have to give up or add? How can I break the pattern to make this fun? When I continue to process a decision in this manner, it never happens that a project won't be fun," he says. "There's always a way out, always a way to make it happen. You see, there is understanding in everything. You put the spin on the ball."

The visualization technique for this week will start you thinking about balance. But imagery isn't the only avenue. Here are some other ways to regain balance and have fun while you're at it. More than likely you do some of these things already but aren't aware why these activities feel so good.

• Organize. When Jim Lea feels himself slipping out of balance, he spends an evening getting organized. "Organization is my way of getting back in control. Once I'm organized, I look to my natural surroundings to regain my balance. I'll ski or cycle or hike or use my quick balance check. My symbol for balance is the sea otter, because he's out there having a great time, but he's getting the job done!"

• Tinker. One president of the Western division of a privately held, top Fortune 100 company slows time to a comfortable pace by tinkering with cars. When he's under the hood of a classic speedster, he loses track of conventional time and sheds his workaday pace.

• Garden. Many people reconnect to their natural rhythms by gardening. Planting obliges us to return to our organic origins. Gardening makes the seasons real again and awakens us to the reality of our cyclical world.

• Processed time—Because computers operate at such incredibly fast speeds, it's easy to lose one's sense of time when working on them. This can have a negative side effect, especially for young children. Educators and child psychologists have observed that children who spend excessive amounts of time playing computer games not only have a less realistic sense of time, they may exhibit more problems relating with others. Used in moderation, however, computers—like any other absorbing activity—can ease stress. One busy plastic surgeon rediscovers his natural rhythms by working on his IBM clone. Plugged into computer time, he loses track of the hours and minutes. By ignoring the clock and concentrating on the screen, he gets up from his desk refreshed and rebalanced.

• Cocooning—Homes are mirrors of our souls. We find clues to balance in cozy rooms, warmed rhythms in a special chair, soothing cycles in a cup that holds a favorite herbal tea. Home nurtures balance in myriad details.

• Music—Music has the power to push us beyond ordinary time. Whether listening to Bach or the Beach Boys, melody soothes and therefore centers us.

• A solitary walk—Walking takes us out of our insulated environments and puts us back on ground level. As we hike or stroll along, we physically establish our own comfortable pace. We absorb and manifest this as a balanced inner tempo.

Think about activities you like to do to relax or reduce stress, and you'll discover other ways to continually readjust your balance.

PAUSE FOR REFLECTION

Here's what you've learned at the end of week two.

1. Determine your image of balance and bring it up frequently.

2. Refer to the chronobiology discussion to become aware of your rhythms.
3. Use the quick balance checks when you are out of sync.
4. When making decisions, measure each significant New Time commitment against your image of balance. Then use the fun factor to double-check!

7

Week Three: Living on Purpose

THE MESSAGE OF THE TAO:
Inner Harmony

Evolved individuals realize that all of their experiences in life are a reflection of their personal cultivation, so they work deeply. They learn to achieve their purpose and master their environment by remaining objective and open to all forms of information.

The *Tao-te Ching* tells us that we detect purpose in life by listening to the inner mind and remaining open to the messages we receive. By deliberately weighing our intuitive reactions against our practical inclinations, we may perceive how the decisions we make concerning time work with or against our purpose.

Instead of looking only to others for guidance, the Tao counsels that we should look inward for direction. Since the answers are within us, we need not accept other people's ideas or systems as our own.

As you begin this inner journey, know that the mind is connected to the universe. Because of this connection, we receive both kinds of signals—cognitive (or external) and intuitive (or internal). To live on purpose, therefore, is to acknowledge all of these messages and honor decisions based on feelings and intuition, as well as those rooted in logic and experience.

106

Key Time Phrase:
How we spend our time defines how we live and who we are.
Key Time Issue:
When priorities evolve from purpose, they cease being a consequence of the clock.
Inner Time Result:
We work always on the most important items and, consequently, we lose our fear of time.
Inner Time Technique:
Staying on purpose by processing right- and left-brain messages.

For this week of deceleration, your focus is purpose—specifically how to live on purpose. The connection between time and purpose should be obvious since how we spend our time determines how we live and who we are. Yet, amazingly, this correlation has been largely overlooked in traditional time management.

The fact is that most of us are put off by purpose. If we're asked to describe our "life purpose," we assume that we are supposed to come up with a lofty comprehensive statement that sums up our entire existence, something inspiring like dedicating ourselves to world peace or solving the problems of the homeless. While some people do have an overwhelming sense of purpose, most of us don't.

If, however, we're asked to identify areas we are repeatedly drawn to, activities or interests that, over the years, give us the most pleasure and satisfaction, most of us would be able to answer this kind of question readily. We may like politics or fashion or learning foreign languages. What we haven't done is recognize that these areas of interest or activity are excellent indicators of purpose—or of subordinate purposes, if you will—that act as directional signals. They carry intuitive messages—triggered by the right side of the brain—that can give us valuable clues to what we are all about.

Living on purpose is nothing more than acknowledging these signals and using them as guides to organize our time.

Many people find that purpose evolves as interests and experiences change. Often we'll follow one path until we've fully explored it, then shift to investigate another avenue. These changes are prompted by continual discovery, conscious or subconscious, of who we are. It is part of the process of growth to peel away layers of ourselves and find new insights.

Don't assume that you can have only one purpose at a time. Many people maintain a main or principal mission along with several subordinate purposes. For example, you may have an overwhelming desire to work with young children. That is your principal purpose, and it shows up repeatedly in your career and personal life. You taught elementary school, ran a program for handicapped children, and now are a mother of a toddler. At the same time, however, you're intrigued by business, fascinated by political change, and have responsibilities to your family and friends that also claim your time and interest.

Although most of us identify purpose with what we do all day—usually our profession—how we spend our time doesn't always indicate that we're living *our* purpose. Too often we make career decisions based on what others expect of us, rather than on what feels right for us. We may also assume mistakenly that how we live indicates what we're all about. But if we're honest with ourselves, life-style, like our career choice, may simply reveal that we've taken the path of least resistance. Because everything in our society pushes us along a predetermined life-style track, most of us go to school, move into the work force, establish our homes, and exit the work force all in predictable fashion. Conditioned to keep up, pressured to perform, we sense an urgency of pace and timing that discourages too much reflection. Consequently, although we organize our daily schedule with care, we don't routinely stop to question whether our intended activities reinforce what we value. It's only during periods when we feel unfulfilled, frustrated, or disappointed that we may pause to wonder whether we are living by default rather than by design.

If living on purpose still sounds like an obscure or impossible order, think about this. Most of us have some sense of ourselves, including some vision of how we would like to be beyond what we are—how we would like to look, what we would choose to do if we had the chance, how much money we would really like to make, and so on. These dreams give us insights as to our direction. But unfortunately, we get so caught up with what we *have* to do, what others *expect* of us and *need* from us, that we don't make *our* vision our priority. Somewhere along the way we lose our sense of what we want, at heart, to be about. This failing helps to explain why our schedules rarely support our sense of purpose.

For the third week of the deceleration program, you'll be working on purpose in three ways. First, you will make a conscious effort to become aware of right-brain messages— messages from the hemisphere of the brain thought to control the emotional and nonanalytical functions. Most time management systems are very left-brain oriented. Although both hemispheres of our brain are always engaged to some degree whenever we think or act, we are conditioned to downplay emotional messages and give credence to our logical and analytical selves. In trying to come to grips with Inner Time, however, the right brain is more operative.

Second, you will evaluate how your decisions involving time support or sabotage your direction. This step, processing both fact and feeling, primes you to receive all kinds of information.

Third, you will include these directional signals as purposeful priorities in your day. This final step, identifying and incorporating purposeful priorities, empowers you to live on purpose.

You use the same period in the morning and evening you devoted to focusing on intentional nows and balance, only this week your assignment is to detect purpose.

MORNING EXERCISE

As with any visualization exercise, find a comfortable place where you will not be interrupted. Sit quietly. Choose any of the relaxation exercises described previously or use one of your own. Calm yourself. Relax deeply.

When you feel completely relaxed, you are ready to begin to visualize purpose.

1. See yourself taking a "time-out" day. Picture the setting in detail. Perhaps you are sitting on a large rock overlooking a lake. Maybe you're relaxing in a favorite chair in a quiet cabin tucked away in the pines. You are spending the day in reflection, taking stock of a specific period in your life. From that period, you think about your accomplishments, the activities you engaged in, what gave you the most satisfaction, what you reacted to negatively, and what aspirations you had.

Day One. Focus on your elementary school years.
Day Two. Concentrate on the years of junior high and high school.
Day Three. Review your college years.
Day Four. Think about your twenties.
Day Five. Move on to your thirties (or review, see below).
Day Six. Your focus is your forties (or review).
Day Seven. Concentrate on your fifties plus (or review).

The scene will change each day as you "age" and as you visualize your time-out day. That's as it should be. Putting yourself in a new place will spark new feelings.

Follow the exercise through your age bracket and then spend whatever remaining days are left this week going back over days one, two, three, and so on. Review your earlier years to see if any new information comes out. There's always more to be discovered.

2. Acknowledge the feelings that arise as you consider each stage of your life. Do you feel happy? Sad? Anxious? Uncertain? Take a moment to let these feelings register. As you consider your activities during each time of life and reflect on how you felt about them, know that your response is a starting point that can lead you in the direction you need to be working on now or can confirm that you are on track.

3. Release the image and leave that time-out scene.

4. Write down the thoughts and feelings you had as you thought back on that time of your life. By acknowledging thoughts *and* feelings, you give credibility to right-brain thinking. These messages are always available to us, but we usually don't listen to them. By quieting the external noises and going within, you encourage intuitive inner messages to come through. For instance, as the week progresses, you may write: "I didn't enjoy sports as a child. I was always picked last." "I loved spending most of my free time in high school riding horses." "I liked to organize events so I joined a lot of clubs." "My first job out of college was the most satisfying, but I thought I had to leave it to move up the corporate ladder." "During this time I joined a small jazz group and played gigs on weekends. It made me realize how much I love having music in my life." By the end of the week you might be making these kinds of observations: "I'm realizing that enjoyment of music and the arts has played a part in every phase of my life." "Ever since I was a kid, money has been my primary passion."

5. Each day, look for common threads that give you clues about purpose. Don't worry if these commonalities don't appear the first few days of visualization. As the week progresses, they will.

6. Reflect on your present situation in light of these insights. For example, the awareness uncovered from the visualization that "Ever since I was a kid, money has been my primary passion" could prompt you to think about money in new ways other than just as income. You could ask yourself if you have incorporated this love of money into the way you

spend your time. Did you choose a career in the financial world? Are you actively involved raising funds for an organization? Does financial planning intrigue you? Do you always find yourself being treasurer of organizations you belong to? If money is a major motivator in your life, it's an indication that it is an innate part of your purpose.

7. Compare the list of long-time interests gleaned from your daily visualization to the way you normally spend your time. As you think about your time commitments, evaluate how your use of time reflects or supports any of the items on your list. Is it in alignment with this list? Is it out of sync? How do you feel about that? If you're not spending sufficient time to support your purpose, even though you are successful by outside standards, you may be unhappy and not able to pinpoint why. For instance, you may have detected through visualization that sports and travel are common threads in much of your life. Yet your job as a computer programmer binds you to your office five days a week. Although you're good at what you do and happy with your job, you feel unfulfilled, even bored.

8. Now turn that list of interests into positive action statements. These become the directional signals to help you stay on course as you plan your day. For example, you may write: "Since I love sports and travel, I'm going to join a cycling club and do some touring on weekends." This statement of intended action becomes a *purposeful priority*.

9. Finally, make a commitment to incorporate purposeful priorities into your life. If this sounds as if you are adding to your already overcrowded day, relax. Besides adding purpose to your life, purposeful priorities act as screening devices to help you sort through new commitments. As you start including purposeful priorities in your life—making time for those activities you love to do or feel a special affinity for—other obligations, second- and third-string things you thought you *had* to do, drop away. Ultimately, as you concentrate on accomplishing your purposeful priorities, you weed out extraneous activities that don't give you as much satisfaction. Know, too, that you can include purposeful priorities daily, weekly, or intermittently. How and when you make time for them is up to you. Just do them.

10. Finish this exercise by making a strong, affirmative statement: "Today my activities will support living on purpose."

To activate this screening process, each day this week, before you agree to take on any new significant activities, check them against your action list of purposeful priorities. Do any of these intended highlights support purpose as expressed by this list? Does your to-do list or daily calendar reflect any of your purposeful priorities? Be aware this week how purpose can act as a force to guide your time.

EVENING PROGRAM

In the evening, repeat the visualization exercise as described. Review your lists from the morning and add any new thoughts that come up.

Resolve to incorporate purpose into your coming day with this affirmation: "*Tomorrow* my activities will support living on purpose."

As you compare your purposeful priorities to the day you just completed, notice how much of the day was devoted to activities that reinforced your direction. How much time were you so caught up in what others expected and demanded of you that you did not work or play on purpose?

As you work on finding direction this week, you may get stuck. Some periods of your life may be easier to tap into than others. Then, too, some days you can be so caught up in external demands—problems, pressures, and deadlines—

that it's difficult for you to concentrate on purpose. What can you do?

Try this clearing technique.

1. Begin by selecting a typical day. Think about how much of your day is spent doing activities that support you.

2. Think about how much of your day is "other directed," filled with self-imposed obligations to the demands of others.

3. Make a list of the "you"-supported activities you are engaged in. How many of these do you consider priorities?

4. Make a list of the other-directed activities. How many of these are priorities?

5. Compare the two lists. If your list of other-directed priorities is longer and more time-consuming than the "you" list, this could be causing your block. You may be feeling so inundated by what others expect of you that you've lost your sense of obligation to yourself.

6. To work out of this block, take the other-directed list and examine it again. Decide whether each item could be altered to support you, whether you can eliminate it entirely, or if that item must remain as is. As you work through the list, keep trying to reduce the other-directed activities until you feel certain that you've done all you can to change them. Notice that as you work through this list, external pressures lessen.

7. When you feel that you've done all that you can to amend the other-directed list, try the visualization again.

LIVING WITH PURPOSEFUL PRIORITIES

It's not easy to stay on purpose. As you look at your day and week, you can't help but notice that you've already made some important and time-consuming commitments. Then, too, you have all those little things biting at your ankles—errands you think you have to do, meetings you assume you must attend. In fact, the more you look at your day and ahead toward the coming week, the more difficult it seems that you will ever be able to stay on purpose.

How do you do it? To make purpose part of your lifetime plan, start by *committing to incorporating just one purposeful priority into your life every day.* As soon as you have uncovered a thread that appears to run through your life, resolve to make it a part of your daily routine. For example, maybe after you've identified sports as a force in your life, you decide to take up cycling. One day you could call various cycling clubs to find out about what's available in your area; the next day you could make a point of checking out riding equipment. The third day you could take a quick warm-up ride or tune up your bike, and so on. By the weekend, you will have taken your first long-distance breakfast ride, met some new friends who share your interest, maybe made a date to ride during the week, and eased into living on this purpose each day.

As you continue living on purpose during the coming weeks, add other activities that support your purposeful priorities. If family is important to you, make a point of calling your mother, taking your son or daughter on a just-for-fun shopping trip or ball game, or taking a leisurely evening walk with your spouse. As you add items that carry out your purposeful priorities, know that you'll probably need to drop other less purposeful activities. To do this, take a hard look at your calendar or to-do list to see what you can eliminate. Do any of the items that you intend to accomplish that day have nothing to do with your purpose as you are understanding it? Can you eliminate any of them? If so, let them go now.

If you feel you cannot relinquish these commitments at this time, decide when you will be able to do so. Whenever possible, give yourself a deadline for letting go.

Finally, as you read over your daily plan, look for purposeful connections. If you dislike board meetings, for instance, but recognize that your commitment to the jazz society is your way of acting out purpose, you may feel better about spending time on something you thought was "extra" or even "time-consuming."

Your ultimate goal is to clear everything off your plate that doesn't support purpose. This won't happen by the end of this week, or even by the end of next month. But it is a practical and worthwhile goal that you can work toward. When all your activities are purposeful, you can be assured that you'll always be focused on what is most important for you.

A Right-Brain Teaser

Sometimes you may have commitments that don't support your purpose, but you don't feel you are ready to let go of them. Your right brain is urging you to release them, but your logical left brain keeps giving you reasons why you should not. In this instance, you may need to tune up the volume of the right-brain messages to encourage you to push beyond the parameters of your everyday thinking.

Try this right-brain strengthener. Reread your list of purposeful priorities. But this time, don't just reread them. Embellish them. See yourself involved in amazing ways with any one of your interests. Choose a common thread and let your imagination soar. Weave a fanciful tapestry, full of color and excitement.

If music excites you, imagine yourself singing *Carmen* at the Met. If you're fascinated by politics, put yourself in the U.S. Senate. If you love the water, be a beach bum. Lead with your interests or passions and then let a silly or outrageous picture emerge. Notice how you feel when you imagine yourself in that situation. And quiet your logical, judgmental side. Costs or talent or other practicalities cannot enter into this at all. Be daring. Have fun.

Repeat this exercise as often as you like during the day.

Start with what feels good to you—or bad—and let your right brain click in and rewrite the scenario so that it gives you pleasure or contentment. Each time you imagine yourself engaged in a wild or crazy activity that supports your purpose, you are reinforcing your commitment to listen to intuitive messages.

Real Life Purpose

If this sounds too outrageous, know that most extremely successful people are driven by original, sometimes outlandish purpose. Larry Wilson, founder of LEAP, knows this as a matter of his own profession. A youthful mid-fiftyish man who exudes energy, Wilson's newest endeavor involves coaching corporate people on how to connect with their purpose. He encourages this breakthrough through a series of carefully orchestrated physical and emotional maneuvers, all choreographed by him and his staff. Still, even Wilson agrees that purpose can be risky business.

"Purpose is what our life is committed to," Wilson offers. "It is not the same as a goal. A goal is something we accomplish within the alignment of purpose. Goals change.

"A farmer plants the seed and then cares for it, but he doesn't control it. He understands that he must wait for the seed to grow. He does all the things necessary to help the seed grow, but he does not make it grow. So, like the farmer, we must learn to do everything necessary to support a process, knowing that we cannot control it.

"Our lives are about letting go of the weeds and old crops, of turning them into energy. Our lives are best accomplished if we know our purpose, our unique talents. Why am I here? To serve? To co-create? To do what? This is the seed.

"Most people are unwilling to come up with a *what* without knowing *how*. But it is perfectly okay *not* to know how as long as you know what. This is really the same as the creative process and not explainable by any scientific means. If a creative idea comes to us out of the blue, as it were, and the ego jumps in and claims credit, then the process stops.

"How do you find the what? You allow it to come through. It's a state we are seldom in."

By visualizing purpose this week and giving your right brain free rein, you are creating that state. You are inviting the "what" to emerge.

So what happens then? That all depends upon who you are. To Scott Alyn, purpose is a specific intention. The thirty-something entrepreneur heads a company called Higher Porpoises, based in Ft. Collins, Colorado. In addition to other products, Higher Porpoises publishes the Elizabeth Kübler-Ross calendar. Alyn is also the artist for that product. He also owns The Great Northwestern Greeting Seed Co. near Portland, Oregon, a small, flourishing company that makes over one hundred different greeting cards containing packets of scented potpourri, teas, bubble baths, or seeds.

Before starting his own business, Alyn was assistant to the marketing director for 7-Up. Although he was successful, he felt a void. "Something was missing," he recounts. "So I set off on a long journey to discover how I could use my business talents and skills in service to something larger than myself." A few years later he was wrestling with another choice—this time between a comfortable corporate position or working on a tree farm for minimum wage. For the first time, he says, he listened to the voice within him that urged him to do what he truly enjoys and to trust that money would come from his positive energy. He chose the tree farm.

Wanting to ensure a long-term livelihood, after work each day Alyn tried to devise a way to combine business experience with his love of nature. Ultimately he planted a large garden at home, thinking "If all else fails, at least I can eat!" A few months later, in the garden, the idea came to him. Why not combine seeds with greeting cards . . . Greeting Seeds®!

Alyn, who has been written up in the *Wall Street Journal* and *Money* magazine, and was recognized by *Megatrends* author John Naisbett for his creativity and success story, says that from the beginning the vision was clear. Although he was turned down by venture capitalists, he now sells more than one million cards a year internationally.

The power of his business is Scott Alyn's purpose. "I hate being driven by outside things," he says. "I want to be internally driven. To do this, I've learned to trust my sense of purpose. It's a specific, not a general intention. My purpose is to bring lightheartedness to the world through my products.

"Purpose for me is an exploration. I filter everything through this sense. My tools for purpose are my journal and writing poetry. Poetry helps me access my purpose, while my journal is my way of visualizing it.

"In thinking over how I relate time and purpose, I've realized that I operate from eight senses. Purpose is my overriding sense, but in addition, I also depend on my sense of place, direction, perspective, order, sense of wonder, beauty, accomplishment, and humor. Each of these are supported by specific activities. For instance, my sense of place is supported by knowing where I live on earth. My tools to do this are rituals to celebrate time and space. Thanksgiving for me is a time to give thanks. I fast because I can't concentrate on giving thanks with a full stomach. Other rituals are my solo backpacking trips and sweat ceremonies that I do.

"My sense of direction is directly connected to purpose. Unless I know what my purpose is, I can't set a direction. My tool here is planning for a month at a time, setting goals and identifying priorities to support my sense of direction. My weekly routine supports my sense of order, and my sense of perspective is supported by the journeys I go on that allow me to step back and get in touch with the cycles that I go through. My sense of accomplishment is supported by celebrations, while my sense of humor is supported through my work and my passion for drawing cartoons, and my sense of beauty and wonder are supported by my love of the outdoors."

Purpose comes through clearly in every department of Scott Alyn's life and business. "My credit and collection department reflects who we are in this company. We send out a card with noodles that says 'Your account is Pasta Due. Please pay-a-uppa or we breaka your noodle.' We have the best collection record of any company, so this is a business aspect as well as a bit of lightheartedness."

Alyn admits that it has taken him years to keep on purpose. To help him stay focused, he screens all information, from incoming mail to appointments and phone calls, searching actively for the purposeful connection.

"Most people find my approach—screening all incoming stimuli to search for quality—refreshing. My approach not only screens for me; it also screens for others," he concludes.

"I pride myself in bringing beautiful, lighthearted, and purposeful products into the world via the marketplace . . . greeting cards that share a gift and help people express emotion, feelings, hopes, and dreams . . . T-shirts that remind us of the preciousness of life, calendars that help us live every day more fully with ourselves and in relationship with others . . . photography that captures the beauty of the earth and reminds us of our role of stewards and that we are only passing through."

By living deliberately and conscientiously on purpose, Alyn says he is always working toward his ultimate goal—simplicity.

Purposeful Prompts

As you concentrate this week on purposeful priorities, here are some more things to think about.

• Talk to yourself about purpose. Twelve years ago singer Diana Ross wrote on her dressing-room mirror FDR's famous quote: "You have nothing to fear but fear itself." Today she has her own quote: "Pick a dream and then work on it. Stay on purpose." Collect quotes that reflect your purpose, or better yet, devise your own. Then repeat that statement frequently.

• Dare to do it all. Yvon Chouinard, founder and chief visionary of Patagonia, the $67-million outdoor-clothing firm, started out making clothes for his own use. He sold handmade clothing out of the back of his car in the late 1950s before setting up shop in a converted meat-packing plant. Chouinard credits his success to taking risks, using common sense, and making good products, but through it all, he's never abandoned his original purpose—to enjoy the outdoors. "My number-one priority is to have free time," Chouinard has stated. Seven months out of the year, he is in some faraway playground—mountain climbing, fishing, kayaking, or wilderness skiing. But he thinks constantly about his company. Those who work with Chouinard point out that he always comes back from his adventures with his best ideas. The Patagonia experience illustrates that regardless of the size and shape of your dreams, you can go for it!

• Request a sabbatical. Many firms today are recognizing the value of taking official time off. IBM, for instance, allows its people to go into VISTA as a means to satisfy deeper needs. Hewlett-Packard pioneered the sabbatical program for top executives to encourage personal renewal. Other companies, like Apple, have followed suit. The finest universities in this country offer their faculties the best sabbatical programs. Inquire whether your company offers such a plan. If you're self-employed, why not plan a sabbatical "on you"?

• Carry a touchstone. To stay in touch with purpose, keep a favorite item in your pocket so that you can touch it during the day to remind you to stay on purpose. Michael Russell always carries a crystal with him, but this contemporary version of "worry beads" can be almost any material. Smooth surfaces are the most soothing to handle, but any such talisman is best for its power of suggestion, not for its material composition.

• Make meaningful contributions. Ben & Jerry's ice cream,

a $45-million-a-year company based in Vermont, gives 7½ percent of its annual profits to charities and has pioneered a "Peace Pop," which carries an advertisement on the stick urging the U.S. Defense Department to spend 1 percent for peace. A purposeful firm, it is dedicated to having fun, being socially responsible, and, according to founder Ben Cohen, "staying weird." To support its sense of fun, Jerry Greenfield heads up the "joy committee." Periodically, he arranges for joyful experiences for employees. To date, Jerry has hired a masseuse to give massages to people on the line, brought in a stand-up comic who entertained people at their desks, and purchased a "synchro-energizer" to help focus energy. (It worked for some people and not for others.) "Our motivation was never to get rich," sums up Ben. "It was to work together." While admitting that as the company continues to grow, he gets more concerned about changing from small to big business, he says optimistically that big-company success can happen "if we pay attention to maintaining our culture, values, and energy, and improving communications."

Cohen happily emphasizes the "weird" part. "The culture of our company is kind of offbeat. We don't follow traditional business paths in terms of marketing or manufacturing or research and development. It also shows up in our relationships. We aren't authoritative or hierarchical. We're fun-loving, loose, and casual."

Think about your own direction as you look over the letters of solicitation you receive, read the countless invitations to charity events, listen to pitches on the telephone, or volunteer to help out organizations. Make a point of supporting only those that suit your purpose. Take care, when you commit your time and resources, to be true to yourself. You'll enjoy the good times more and weather the difficult moments more easily.

• Use purpose to work smarter. Identify areas where your purpose and the company's mission merge to strengthen your sense of personal purpose and help you work more effectively.

If you are considering a new job, a "purposeful fit" is something you should consider. In an existing job, seeking out commonalities can help you find logical and most effective places to begin selling yourself. If you're committed to social betterment, for example, you could consider making use of your knowledge of Spanish by starting a company class on English for Spanish-speaking employees of your firm; or you could volunteer to head a corporate drive to aid homeless children. In such instances, although you are working from your own higher purpose, it's a good bet that your efforts won't go unnoticed by your company.

• Leaving on purpose. One Chicago woman who had spent five years in the corporate travel business recalls that when she finally acknowledged what was happening to her career, it was a painful confrontation. "As I became unhappier, I ultimately saw that the others in my business were in it for entirely different reasons than I was. Not only were our goals and objectives different, but we were working at cross-purposes. I initially interpreted this as a failure on my part, that I should have known better or hadn't done things right. It was extremely traumatic for me until I could sort it out." Although she was devastated when she left that firm, after comparing her purpose with those of the others involved in the business, she was able to start the healing process. Today this forty-three-year-old executive has a flourishing corporate consulting firm specializing in producing industrial meetings for corporations, including sports-related industries. Her new business supports her need to be in control of her own destiny and combines her love of entertainment and sports with her desire for travel.

• Write a personal mission statement. Although most successful corporations have mission statements, few individuals ever write these down. Bill Pelder, co-founder of Mainstream Access, a New York–based firm that specializes in corporate reorganization and renewal, suggests that one way to do this is to take a sheet of paper and put four headings on it: family;

friends; business; church and/or community. Using these headings as guides, think about what you would like to have said about you at your own funeral. A mission statement should be a clear, concise summary that illustrates what is important to you.

• Indulge the best of your past. As you visualize various stages of your life this week, help yourself along by rereading old letters, calling a dear friend you rarely see, leafing through scrapbooks, or listening to favorite old songs. Such diversions can help you prime the pump and sharpen your recall. If you are interested in exploring the concept of purpose further, many books have been written on this subject. You can also attend seminars devoted to life purpose. An excellent place to begin this search is your local library or bookstore.

A Few More Thoughts

Making a living is one thing. Making a living worthwhile is another.

Joe Stacey,
former editor of
Arizona Highways Magazine

I am lucky because I live my life purpose minute by minute. It is not altogether luck because I did go within and find it. This strong calling comes from the depth of my being. When my children gave me a fiftieth birthday party, they told me that I gave them the most wonderful gift—a model of a life that has meaning.

Barbara Marx Hubbard

Without a firm idea of himself and the purpose of his life, man cannot live and would sooner destroy himself than remain on earth, even if he was surrounded with bread.

Dostoyevski

Our real journey in life is interior; it is a matter of growth, deepening, and of ever greater surrender to the creative action of love and grace in our hearts.

Thomas Merton

PAUSE FOR REFLECTION

At the end of week three, you've learned how to:

1. Tune in and listen to right-brain messages.
2. Recognize directional signals—common threads of activities and interests that indicate purpose.
3. Turn these directional signals into purposeful priorities.
4. Commit to making purposeful priorities a regular part of your life.

8

Week Four:
Conscious Choice as a Life Force

THE MESSAGE OF THE TAO:
Steady force of
attitude and return to simplicity

Essential to the notion of conscious choice is an understanding that *you* are your most powerful time management tool. Only you can make decisions as to how and when you will spend your time. You have the ability to make choices that reflect what you want to be about, or you can abdicate this responsibility and be swept along by the tide of events. While notebooks, organizers, and to-do lists are all handy tools that can help you carry out your decisions, none of these external items is the mobilizing force. That is you—your inner being.

This belief in *you* as a force for action is Taoist in intent. The way of the Tao teaches that your beliefs create your reality. How you think and feel about your day and surroundings and schedule are manifested in your life. The Tao also points out that if you search out the positive in all things, you will find it, whereas if you dwell on the negative, negative forces will continue to plague you. Therefore, one of the axioms of Taoist philosophy is that since your reality is largely determined by your attitude, you have the power to create your life as you wish it to be.

Having recognized that conscious choice is a powerful conduit for life force, how do we activate it to help us design our way of time? To take this final step, we turn again to the Taoist teachings for guidance. The teachings advocate an achieved simplicity. Simplifying time in your life means reducing decisions to a simple "yes" or "no." To do this, you must be open to hearing both your logical and intuitive selves, willing to accept whatever outcome is indicated, and, finally, able to embrace the reality of the hidden world as freely as you accept the revealed environment. Only by accepting both can you know the harmony and ultimate simplicity of being in accord.

Key Time Phrase:
We have the power to use time in the way we choose.
Key Time Issue:
Making conscious choices eliminates the negative connotations of time, thus eliminating self-induced pressures.
Inner Time Result:
Conscious choice simplifies our use of time.
Inner Time Technique:
Reducing the complexity of decisions to a simple "yes" or "no."

Until now the focus of this program has been directed at making the time you spend more meaningful, because as activities grow in purpose they become less dependent on time.

For the first three weeks of this program, we've approached this goal in three ways. First we concentrated on creating intentional now moments. Then we added the personal element of rhythms and balance. Next we delved deeper by identifying purposeful connections that you could begin to incorporate into your day. Throughout these weeks, we stressed concentration on the highlights of your day since, if your most significant activities are in alignment with your rhythms and purpose, these positive feelings will carry over into other aspects of your life. Each of these steps has helped you move away from your dependence on the clock and toward an awakening to Inner Time.

Now, with conscious choice, we move into the hands-on phase of deceleration. Conscious choice is nothing more than making deliberate decisions based on spontaneous but directed inquiry.

There is a direct relationship between decision making and time. Not only is much of our time spent making, living with, and agonizing over our decisions, but once we decide to do something, we often attach a time frame to it. When we put a time limit on an action, we create additional pressure for ourselves. Now not only are we committed to a decision, we also may feel constrained by the clock. This perceived pressure is often what puts us in a race against time.

In contrast, when we use the Inner Time technique described in this chapter to make decisions, we eliminate this self-induced pressure of racing against the clock.

For this week, you'll practice distilling the process of decision making to a simple "yes" or "no." This is a powerful technique. It can be used to interrupt habitual behavior, stop overload, eliminate overcorrecting your course of action, and help you get past the fear of taking either positive or negative action. The yes/no format is both simple and profound. With it you put your inner voice on the line.

Inner voice comes to us as thought. Thought is not generated in the outer workings of the mind, but rather emanates from the interior depth of our being. Committing to listen to this voice requires a staunch and steady belief in one's own power. To do this you must willingly enter into the hidden mental world that underlies existence.

Like time itself, the power of that hidden world is limitless. Albert Schweitzer once remarked, "The greatest discovery of any generation is that human beings can alter their lives by altering their attitudes of mind." The entire premise of the deceleration program is that you can alter your way of time by choosing to change your attitude about time.

None of us lives a choiceless life. Every day, every moment we are faced with decisions. Should we finish this report or break for coffee? Should we eat that doughnut or resist it? Should we call him ... or wait and hope that he will call? Nearly every waking moment we are confronted with all sizes and conditions of decisions. Some we accept involuntarily; others we make intentionally. But even during those times when we are deliberately selecting among options, we may not be making conscious choices so much as choosing among ready-made alternatives. If we stopped to examine the process closely, we might be forced to concede that we are not choosing freely but rather are selecting from a menu we have never chosen in the first place.

Part of our dilemma is that decisions are rarely clear-cut. We have conditions to consider, feelings to satisfy, a forest of "what ifs" to cut through. By the time we weigh all our options, it's easy to get tangled up in what others expect. Because we don't want to offend, we bend. Because we have pride—of course we can do it!—we ignore our innate warning signals. Unwilling to disappoint an employer or co-worker, family member or friend, we push ahead, silencing our inner voice. We take on added responsibilities ... we agree to additional work ... we accept extra assignments ... when all the while we hear that whisper—"Enough!" Conscious choice grants us permission to say—as our mothers have told us—"enough is enough."

While many blocks can hinder our ability to make conscious choices, the following five are the most common culprits.

The first block is *habit*. We are habitual creatures, and as long as we can get away with it, we tend to do things the same way again and again and again. Although we may talk about starting over, usually we don't. It's easier to follow a well-worn path than to forge a new one. So, whether choosing a restaurant, selecting a doctor, or determining who will head a project, when faced with choices we generally lean toward the familiar rather than stretching to consider new options. We react automatically instead of thinking through all possibilities. Although some habits are convenient—do we really want to stop and ponder for five minutes when choosing one brand of coffee over another?—many are limiting. Making conscious choices interrupts habitual behavior.

Overload is the second obstruction to decision making. When you feel overwhelmed, everything seems more difficult—especially making intelligent choices. When we have heaps of things hanging over our heads—all with clocks ticking—we don't think clearly. Instead, we feel the crunch of time.

We get overloaded because we've been taught both to fill our plates and clean them, whether we're dealing with a dinner or an agenda. Because in our society we equate self-worth with work, we inundate ourselves with responsibilities. If we do it all, we prove ourselves. Recognizing that overload is a real impediment to clear decision making is the first step to overcoming this common block.

A third barrier to conscious choice is *course correction*—going into a decision presuming that you can change your mind. Course correction complicates decision making because it can turn a simple process into an ordeal.

There are many times when correcting your course of action is a positive and necessary move. You make a decision based on information that seems right at that moment. But within a short time, it becomes apparent that you need to change direction. Being flexible enough to recognize that you need to change—and making that change—is not only admirable, it can save you from serious trouble. However, if you fall into the trap of *expecting* to correct your course, not only do you surrender your power to choose, you never really commit.

The fourth and fifth common obstructions to conscious choice are *fear of saying "no"* and *fear of saying "yes."* Just as is the case when we depend excessively on course correction, whenever we say "yes" or "no" out of fear, we assume a powerless position.

For many people, saying "no" is a traumatic experience. A colleague requires help. The boss hands out a rush assignment. A student urgently needs your time. How can you refuse? Because you have difficulty saying "no," you say "yes." Afraid to commit positively, you give away your power.

The same holds true for saying "yes." Often we erect this block because we aren't certain about the outcome of a decision. We may worry that we won't perform adequately, or we're fearful that we don't fully understand all the consequences of an action. Because we are afraid to give an affirmative response, we refuse and thereby abdicate our power.

Underlying every block to effective decision making is one other overriding fear—the fear of making a mistake. As you learn to use the Inner Time technique described in this chapter when making significant choices, you'll see that this concern will diminish as your sense of personal power grows.

Realistically, when you begin to make conscious choice a part of your life, you cannot stop to question every situation you are faced with. If you did, you'd soon feel stymied and even paralyzed. However, as you practice the Inner Time technique of yes/no, it will become easier and more natural for you to approach decision making in this manner. Gradually you'll begin to unravel complex choices instinctively, or to frame questions that require decisions so routinely that they may be easily answered by a simple but powerful "yes" or "no." As you become proficient at this technique, you'll see how making decisions in this manner simplifies your use of time.

Before you begin, understand, however, that no decision-making approach can guarantee that you'll always be delighted with the outcome. But what you can count on is the satisfaction you'll have of knowing that you saw your options clearly, were open to accept the answer, and steered your destiny to the best of your ability.

VISUALIZING SIMPLICITY

For the fourth week of deceleration, use the same fifteen minutes morning and evening you've been devoting to visualizing intentional nows, balance, and purpose, but this week concentrate on conscious choice.

Begin by relaxing. Use the circular deep breathing technique described in chapter 6. Take as many deep, circular breaths as you need to until you feel yourself calming and slowing down. You will probably find that relaxation comes easily and more naturally for you by this fourth week of the program.

When you feel at ease and at peace, begin with this visualization.

MORNING VISUALIZATION

1. See yourself ready to start today's activities with the power to choose what activities you will do, as well as when and how you will complete them. To assure that you are beginning from a position of power, clean your mental slate of any thoughts of "must dos" and "have tos" and "what ifs" and concentrate on feeling power. Although this is an extremely individual sensation, it's been described as feeling supremely confident, knowing you're right, seeing clearly, having no doubts. To summon this powerful impression, it may help to picture yourself in a place of power—sitting on top of a mountain or even on a throne.

2. Once you have created an image of your powerful self, focus on one activity you are going to engage in today that requires a decision on your part or involves a question that must be resolved.

3. Picture yourself eliminating any blocks you may have to making a choice concerning that activity. You may find it helpful to imagine these blocks as physically encircling your decision. If any habitual behavior is getting in the way of your making this choice, tip over that block.

Check for feelings of overload. If you are feeling inundated, that's another block. Push it out of the circle. As you do so, feel your mind clear.

As you consider this decision, can you commit wholeheartedly to it? Or do you expect to change your mind once you make a choice? If excessive course correction is a problem for you, push that block aside as well. Feel the fresh air that flows through the circle.

Finally, be honest about your ability to say "yes" or "no." If either of these tendencies hinders you, physically remove it from your circle by pushing either or both of those fearful blocks aside.

4. Now, with your choice fully exposed, state your question concerning this issue so that it can be answered with a simple "yes" or "no." Be careful not to include any expectations in your statement. Phrase the question simply and directly. Give yourself a few moments to experience the question. Ask for the answer.

5. Allow the thought of the answer to float to your consciousness. Feel the power within you as you ask for guidance from this totally relaxed state.

6. If you do not receive an answer, accept this as well. Do not feel pressured to force a decision. Be assured that the answer will come when the time is right. Repeat that question again in the evening.

7. Complete the visualization with this affirmation: "Today I allow myself the freedom to choose what, when, and how I will use my time."

EVENING VISUALIZATION

• Repeat the relaxation exercise. Picture yourself in a powerful position. See yourself ready to start tomorrow's activities. If you received the answer to your morning question, select a different activity that will require your decision tomorrow. If you have not clearly heard a "yes" or "no," repeat the morning image.

• Each morning and each evening, if you have resolved the previous question, focus on a new activity that requires a decision.

• During the day, frequently focus on the powerful picture or image you created with your most recent visualization.

• Use the affirmation often. Whenever you are faced with any decision during the day, repeat the affirmation first to remind you of your personal power. Then make your choice.

GETTING UNSTUCK AND BACK ON TRACK

If making decisions quickly is difficult for you, occasionally you may become blocked when trying to do this visualization exercise—even when visualizing the "removal" of the blocks. If this happens, don't get upset. Instead, try to relax again. If you still can't get the juices flowing, reach for a sheet of paper and a pencil and get to work on those barriers.

1. Begin by listing some of the common blocks you carry around with you. All of us have some baggage that we must deal with. Maybe you have difficulty making decisions because you feel that you must live up to others' expectations. Perhaps your old habits get in the way. If you often feel overcommitted and therefore overwhelmed, appreciate that during these times you can't think as clearly as you should. Possibly you've gotten into the habit of jumping into situations quickly, only to find that they don't turn out to be what you expected. Then you spend a lot of time and energy backpedaling and rearranging. Or perhaps, if you're honest with yourself, you'll admit you have trouble saying "yes" or "no."

2. After identifying your blocks, reread your list.

3. Ask yourself: "Can I let go of them?" If you answer "yes," decide when and how you plan to eliminate each barrier. For instance, you may decide that as of Friday, you'll make a concerted effort to stop overloading yourself with extra work.

4. Once you've identified your plan of action, return to the visualization.

5. If you answer "no"—that you can't let go of what is blocking you at this time—write down why you're unwilling to release that block. You might confess that your basic insecurity about your career or your bank account is what drives you to accept all jobs—even those you know you won't like. Or you may discover that you intentionally create chaos because your penchant for keeping those around you confused gives you an illusion of being in control.

6. Now ask yourself, "Why do I render myself powerless?"

This isn't an easy question to answer. As you mull it over, face up to the fact that you cannot change your attitude about time and decision making until you work through this question of *why* you render yourself powerless. First you need to confront the problem. Only then can you begin to understand why you have difficulty making decisions. Until you can discover why you are unwilling to let go of your blocks and release this counterproductive attitude, you won't be able to gather your power and make choices easily. As you work this week at trying to unblock, coming to terms with the question of powerlessness may be the most difficult choice of all.

PRACTICAL CHOICES

Although the yes/no technique depends heavily on right-brain thinking, conscious choices aren't made off the cuff. While hunches may pay off, this technique is successful only when you are clearly ready to make a choice. Being ready usually means that you've done your homework, assembled the facts, and know your alternatives.

All this can take time.

Taking time in our society isn't easy—not when everything in our accelerated culture pushes us to move along and make fast decisions so that we don't hold up the parade. When time is of the essence—especially when time is money—no one likes to wait. In decelerated decision making, waiting is an essential part of the process. Your inner voice won't be rushed. Because you cannot hurry thought, you receive answers to your questions only when the time is right.

If you accept the Taoist premise that *you* are your most powerful source of time and action, you know that you can recognize when the time is right. Until then, you also must be prepared to wait. There is a natural gestation period for making decisions that cannot be forced. Until the decision is ripe for the picking, "time out" is not only indicated, it's imperative.

Having gathered your own power, you still have to deal with the rest of the world—a partner who is breathing down your neck to get an answer, a superior who is demanding a response, a spouse who is quickly losing patience. What do you do?

The only difference between conscious choice and traditional decision making is that with Inner Time you make decisions from the inside out. You begin by tuning into your own inner signals to hear what's right for you rather than immediately trying to please or ameliorate all factions. When you come to decision making from this powerful perspective, you will feel confident of your ability to know when to take action and when to wait for more information.

At times you may get a clear "Yes . . . but" or a "No, but if I wait . . ." Pay attention to these signals and never try to force the issue. What this message is saying is that you don't have all the evidence yet. You need to wait. If this is irritating and discomfiting to you, keep in mind that while you cannot make a career out of never deciding, neither can you build a solid career on making decisions before their time.

Many people will warn you that if you don't decide right away, you are taking negative action; or put another way, that by not taking action you are condoning the status quo. Be aware that most decisions are not *that* urgent. Very few things in this world must be decided instantly. If you receive these urgent messages, put them into perspective. Consider the messenger. Say it's a business colleague. Is she demanding the answer because it's vital to the well-being or survival of the business, or because it's vital to her? Or is she trying to push a decision simply because it's more convenient for her to know the answer?

Take comfort in knowing that most of us—even dedicated procrastinators—will sooner rush into any decision than let it get dangerously overripe.

The more comfortable you get using the yes/no technique, the more others will pick up on your confidence. Although your friends and colleagues may never adjust their work style to yours, given time and your example they'll come to appreciate that you are not only serious in this approach to making choices, you are also successful. What initially may have been seen as indecisiveness on your part eventually will be appreciated as deliberate, intuitive thinking.

TOSSED COINS
AND CONSCIOUS CHOICES

Wayne Silby is the founder and CEO of the Calvert Group, an investment firm with more than $2 billion in funds. Silby started the business in 1977 with a partner. "One of our funds is devoted to making investments that support a social consciousness," he says. "While lots of our funds are pretty traditional, this is the one we're best known for. It's interesting that when I came up with this idea, my vision for this fund was so strong that I overrode my management team, who was not in favor of it."

Semiretired at age forty for three years (he still assumes an overview of the Calvert Group), Silby is a success by anyone's standards. And what really makes him unusual in his world is his approach to decision making. Back in the late sixties, as a young college graduate, he did some traveling in India. Although he returned to the States and went to law school, some of the spirituality stuck.

"A number of years later, when we had started the Calvert Group, our management team was looking for a symbol," he recalls. "We were young; we had no contacts. We relied on sheer strategy."

Silby suggested that they select their symbol out of the *I Ching,* a Chinese book of wisdom closely related to the *Tao-te Ching.* "We were hiring a systems analyst who had just come back from China," he continues. "She had a copy of the text in Chinese and said she would come and read from it. I had our managers with me and we each did a roll of the coins. Each of us rolled a straight line, which is the first— and most powerful—symbol of the *I Ching.* What really was amazing was that our systems analyst said that she dreamed the previous night that we all would roll that symbol."

Since that time, every year his management team rolls the coins and asks for guidance. "It's not cause and effect," he cautions, "as much as parallels or coincidence that we uncover. The patterns are there waiting to be discovered. You don't create the patterns, you find what exists just below the surface. The *I Ching* is not an oracle. It doesn't give answers. It provokes you to understand."

Today Silby rolls the coins only a few times a year to ask

for deep guidance. For less serious but still significant decision making, this financial whiz uses a flotation tank, an apparatus like an oversized, enclosed bathtub in which you sit or float buoyed by water and surrounded by silence. Although these costly tanks are not as widely available as they once were, they are produced both for home and commercial use. "You concentrate on the problem before you go into the tank," Silby says. "Then when you're submerged, you think about nothing. That's harder to do than you may suspect. As you lie there, the answer bubbles to the surface."

When he doesn't use the coins or the tank, Silby depends on his intuitive nature. Specifically, he explains, "I actually put off decisions until I cannot do so any longer. Good decision making includes hanging in there—in a state of confusion. It's a male ethos that good decisions are clear, that if you don't know what to do, it's a sign of weakness. Sometimes maybe it is, but I think that it's right and proper to be confused. I give time to this state.

"During this period you feel uncomfortable. You may feel stupid. Many people would rather make some decision than submit to this complicated and frustrated period. But I believe one of the most underrated decisions in the investment business is deciding when to wait—when to do nothing. Some of the best investment people in the business make one or two decisions a year and spend the rest of the time waiting. You have to recognize your bias toward wanting to make something happen, listen quietly, and wait. The best decisions are the ones that you cannot *not* make.

"It's important for executives and management teams to make it okay for people to be confused for a certain period of time, to allow them time to work through the confusion to arrive at an answer. It's my experience that most people don't hang in there long enough."

Silby depends on this approach to decision making in his personal life as well. "When my wife and I go shopping, it's like an ordeal," he admits. "I use this same approach to buying a pair of pants. I sometimes waste time on decisions that aren't that important.

"In business I'll agonize over whether to see a person on Sunday or Monday. I can take almost anything and tear it apart. I did the same thing when I was deciding to get married. I went through all the downside, all the tests. I thoroughly kicked the tires. Some people, in this situation, put their best foot forward. Not me. But once we made the decision to get married I focused everything I had on supporting that decision and making it work. There's no value in looking back. If something starts not to work, you can change it if need be. But then, that's just another decision you have to make."

What kind of reaction does Silby get to his deliberate style of conscious decision making? "Sometimes I get involved with businessmen who I feel a little hustle from," he acknowledges, "but I made a decision a long time ago that I have to do things at my own style and pace. I've seen situations where people have been forced into making decisions faster than they were comfortable with, and most of the time they would have been better off if they hadn't made that choice.

"Most of us aren't that quick. Not all of us are able to see the obvious. So if you can't come from being yourself in making decisions, you're headed for trouble. I don't think you have an option other than to be yourself and do things at your own pace and style."

He pauses for a moment to frame his thoughts. "You know, there's this saying that in America we take one day to make a decision and ninety-nine days to implement it. In Japan, they take ninety-nine days to make a decision, and they implement it in one day."

PUMPING UP YOUR POWER

The effectiveness of the Inner Time technique of yes/no is dependent on your ability to summon your personal power.

Gathering power gives you the steady force of attitude that's needed to make conscious choices.

If personal power is a new concept for you, it may help you this week to contemplate a "power profile." Although our traditional definition of power implies wealth, fame, and influence, "true power" is quite a different matter.

People who have true power are unconcerned with the impression they make. They are more interested in the person they are. They find that their sense of inner peace increases constantly.

A truly influential person is someone who can—and does—direct his will to a higher good. His sense of power is palpable and catching. When you are in the company of a person with true power, regardless of the topic of conversation, you come away feeling that you have gained access to a deeper level of being.

True power is seen in a person's eyes. There is love in the eyes of those who are truly powerful. They look at you directly. They don't avoid your gaze. They pay attention to what *you* are saying and you feel recharged and regenerated from being in their company.

Powerful people do not attempt to convince you of anything. They only invite and offer. They never persuade or manipulate. They don't use aggression to get their way.

Instead, they listen. If they can offer you anything they sense that you need, they do so. If not, they offer you attentive, wholly committed silence.

During week four of deceleration, look around for role models of people who are truly powerful. Notice how others react to them. This won't be difficult to do, for truly powerful people give off distinctive signals. Brooke Newell, a former Wall Street banker who is now a consultant to businesses and industries undergoing drastic reorganizations, has long been practicing New Time techniques. She exudes a calm, quiet strength, which she attributes to her philosophy about time and herself. Newell, who believes that "our inner essence determines the outer form," acknowledges, "People often notice that there is something different about me."

A QUICK AND INTENSIVE
ENERGY TECHNIQUE

Sometimes you need a dose of quick energy to help you stay committed to a choice you've made. Making the decision is one thing; implementing it is another. For example, you've made a decision to hire a new buyer and you feel positive about your choice. But you start running into problems almost immediately. After wrangling on the telephone for three days with him over everything from his title to the color of carpet in his office, you're ready to pack it in and admit that you can't reach a satisfactory agreement. Despite your initial clear and positive signal to hire this person, you begin to doubt your decision. In this case, an energizing visualization can make the difference between staying committed and giving up.

Sports psychologists have long used various intensive visualization techniques to pull peak performances out of athletes. One top United States woman cyclist who rides for the Weight Watchers women's team confides that she routinely visualizes before each race. "First I relax by visualizing a special scene," she says. "Then I see and hear and feel myself crossing that finish line first. I actually see my wheel cross over the line and I feel the win."

Athletes know that, with practice, they can tap into this almost superhuman power to summon energy on demand. You can use this source to help you carry through on those conscious decisions. Suppose you've made a choice to ask your boss for a raise, but you get cold feet at the thought of walking in and facing him. Or perhaps you've agreed to chair the annual fund-raising event for the art museum, but as you start making calls and run into a noticeable lack of enthusiasm you start to wonder if you were crazy to take the job.

To gather a short-term, high-impact burst of energy, visualize a thought, feeling, or sound (using the visualizing exercises given earlier in this chapter) that pumps you up, an image or sensation that causes your adrenaline to flow. Give yourself some time to come up with this image; it must feel right for you to be effective. Once you've chosen the sight or sound or feeling that triggers your emotional and physiological response, embellish it. Fill in all the details. Make this image as vivid as you can.

One sports psychologist who successfully employs this technique has reported that a professional ice skater he works with always imagines swallowing a star and having it burst inside her, infusing her body from head to toe with spreading energy, before she heads onto the ice in competition.

Once you have this energizing image, concentrate on it for a few moments each day. Bring up this image whenever you need to get "turbocharged" to get through a doubting or difficult time.

Don't be shy about adding sound effects. Gambling casinos use sight and sound to pump up patrons. Slot machines are programmed so that the rhythmic jingle of the coins paying off acts like jungle drums, inciting people to action. Flashing lights and bells reinforce the mounting excitement. If you have a sound that rings your bells, use it to gather your forces.

Feelings are equally potent energizers. Remember what it felt like to paddle your own kayak through a river rapid? Or the exhilaration of being the high scorer in a basketball game? If you can identify a feeling that thrills you physically and emotionally, put it in your arsenal.

Use this same visualizing technique for calming yourself. Many decisions require cool stick-to-itiveness in the face of rising panic. To help you stay committed to your yes/no choice, select a sight or sound or feeling that says "calm" or "tranquillity" to you. You may find it helpful to go to nature for this picture. A placid pool with ripples emanating from

the center . . . the silence of a winter snowfall . . . the feeling
you experience when you see green shoots poking through
the earth in spring.

Quick energizers and calmers can help you implement
your conscious choices.

SOME AFFIRMATIONS
ABOUT POWER

People have described the feeling of using the yes/no technique in various ways. It's been identified as extra recognition,
revelation, a sixth sense, a feeling in the bones, insight,
hunches or gut reactions, a way to get past the Y in the road.
Astronaut Edgar Mitchell refers to it as "active meditation,"
a process that, he says, forces you to confront and deal with
your reality.

Barbara Marx Hubbard says she uses the principle of conscious choice constantly in her approach to time. "Whenever
I feel a moment of anxiety when making a decision, I process
it until I can dissolve what's causing it. After a while, if you
do this enough, you develop a spiritual muscle."

Asked to describe her approach to decision making, a
California freelance advertising and marketing woman wrote,
"More and more I consciously make choices about my use of
time. As I've grown older, I've realized that my time *is* my
life and that for the most part I make the choices about the
use of my time. I use my time effectively by first deciding
what I want. For example, I want to raise my son and help
him to learn what life has to offer. I want him to learn what
has true value in life and what doesn't. To do this, I must
take quality time with him to build a strong, loving relationship and to teach him. I, in turn, am able to learn about
myself from him. To me, quality time means being able to
apply your full attention to whatever you're involved in at
that moment."

"Let go. Trust. Be patient. Let life unfold. Don't force decisions. You know when everything is right to make a choice," says Brooke Newell. Although Newell says she tries to make conscious decisions, she admits that sometimes she still runs on automatic. "Still," she says with a smile, "the more I do this, the better it is."

If you have difficulty letting go, difficulty trusting and allowing decisions to emerge naturally, try this easy and fun exercise. This week, each day, take a decision that you need to make that isn't life-determining. You might choose where you'll eat lunch or which entree to order. Narrow your choices down to two. Instead of making a conscious choice, flip a coin.

Flipping a coin is an easy way to release mental blocks to decision making because you physically "let go" of the decision and give it up to chance. Moreover, this simple technique should help you see that many decisions do not require a complicated approach to problem solving.

PAUSE FOR REFLECTION

At the end of week four you have:

1. Become aware of five common blocks that create time pressures.
2. Acknowledged that the inner voice is the powerful force behind all your decisions.
3. Seen how the yes/no technique simplifies your use of time.
4. Learned that it's okay to wait.

9

Weeks Five, Six, and Beyond: Designing Your Time

THE MESSAGE OF THE TAO:
Self-Mastery

Those who know others are intelligent;
Those who know themselves have insight.
Those who master others have force;
Those who master themselves have strength.

Those who know what is enough are wealthy.
Those who persevere have direction.
Those who maintain their position endure.
And those who die and yet do not perish, live on.

Self-knowledge and self-mastery are the primary Taoist accomplishments. These are achieved when an individual cultivates the inner mind, refining instincts and intuitive responses to the world. The result of this cultivation is insight—the ability to perceive the larger influences behind specific social phenomena.

As R. L. Wing concludes, to know the inner mind and perceive its connection with the evolving mind of the universe forms the foundation for lifelong learning. Through inner knowledge, one develops the ability to alter the world through small, steady, effortless actions that take place at the very beginning of events. Those who "die and yet do not perish" are those who leave the affairs of the world in a more evolved state than when they encountered them.

Self-mastery is essential to understanding and using the principles of Inner Time. As you consider the work that lies ahead of you to achieve this goal, know that your perseverance will be rewarded. By following the steps, not only will you lose much of the sense of pressure that often accompanies the clock, you will also put into place a continuing process of personal growth. Like time, that process is limitless. The evolution will continue as long as you remain committed to the principles of Inner Time.

Ultimately you will become part of that directed congregation who contribute to the evolved state of the world, for as you design your way of time, you will also gain an understanding of the universe and of the higher, natural order that exists within it.

The four steps you have practiced over the last four weeks provide you with the techniques to begin this journey. Along the way, each day you will gain more insight into your relationship with time. Insight into time is not the gift of any "system." It may be found only by quieting the external noises and listening to the voice of the inner mind.

Key Time Phrase:
Designing our time allows us to define our own pace and relationship to time.

Key Time Issue:
Responding to internal cues frees one from focusing on the "when" of time and eliminates the accelerated pace defined by the clock.

Inner Time Result:
We create our own sense of time.

Inner Time Technique:
Three self-centering questions to plan your day.

Here is where you'll put it all together to design your own way of time. You've got all the pieces. You are comfortable living in the now. You can go within for balance and are sensitive to your rhythms. You are aware how purposeful priorities can help you align your time with your purpose. And you've learned how to make conscious choices about your time rather than rely on automatic or habitual decisions.

With this final exercise, you will synthesize the preceding four steps into a single visualization and affirmation. You'll use the morning and evening visualizations until they become so automatic for you that decelerating is second nature.

Although the principles are presented as a six-week program, the timetable for deceleration is completely flexible. Don't feel bound by it. And please, do not move on to this final step until you feel completely comfortable with all four previous principles. This is the time to be totally honest. How do you feel about your ability to create intentional nows? Can you check your balance easily? Are you identifying and making time for purposeful priorities? What about your decision-making skills? Are you making conscious choices about the important things in your life, or do you find that you fall back into old patterns?

If you aren't completely at ease with all of these steps, go back now and spend more time on the specific visualizations that aren't coming naturally to you. It's not possible to master the final, synthesizing exercise until the Inner Time foundation is firmly in place.

Remember, too, that your focus with these four steps is directed toward the *most important* items or highlights that you choose to accomplish during your day. In this respect, as you create intentional nows, maintain balance, set purposeful priorities, and make conscious choices, you are drafting a general plan for those key activities, those old As and Bs that you used to struggle with. As you put these steps together, don't get sidetracked by the myriad demands that you know will come up in your day. You'll handle those in the next section. There you'll get a new arsenal to use—specific visualizations to combat sabotaging, time-intensive problems that can stop you in your tracks.

With all this in mind, let's move on to connecting the four steps.

The overriding principle of Inner Time is that you can connect your power with the energy of unlimited universal time. To forge this link, you must review and master one more concept—the Taoist-inspired idea of being, doing, and having.

The secret is in the sequencing. Shakti Gawain in *Creative Visualization* explains being, doing, and having this way.

You can think of life as containing three levels. We call these levels beingness, doingness and havingness. Beingness is the basic experience of being alive and conscious. It is the experience we have in deep meditation, the experience of being totally complete and at rest within oneself.

Doingness is movement and activity. It stems from the natural creative energy that flows through every living thing and is the source of our vitality.

Havingness is the state of being in relationship with other people and things in the universe. It is the ability to allow and accept things and people into our lives, to comfortably occupy the same space with them. . . . They are not in conflict with each other and they all exist simultaneously.

Westerners often have it backward. In traditional time management courses, you are urged to begin with what you want to *have*. Then you decide what you must *do* in order to achieve it. When the emphasis is on immediate problem solving rather than on personal growth, *being* is never introduced. While with these methods you may alleviate some time pressures temporarily, because your state of being is not affected, you never generate any deep or lasting changes in how you view and interact with time. True, you may appear more in control to others, but it's a cosmetic rather than a reconstructive difference. Ultimately you return to your old ways, and with new frustration.

To understand and accept an inner-directed approach to time, we begin by connecting to our state of being in time, which, in turn, helps us focus and facilitate what we do every day, which then allows us to have the unlimited view of time that we desire.

For the final two weeks of the program, you'll be concentrating on making these concluding exercises a permanent image in your mind. You'll know when you have mastered them, because you'll be able to recall the morning and evening visualization easily and effortlessly.

Only after you feel secure that you have this visualization firmly in your mind should you move ahead to the final, culminating step: eliminating all the exercises entirely. Instead of consciously running through any visualization as you plan your day or consider a request for your time, you will tap into the essence of the exercise to recall the mental checklist of the four steps—now, balance or centering, purpose, and conscious choice—and the three self-centering questions you'll learn in this synthesizing step. These questions are introduced in the following morning visualization (step 6). The checklist and the questions become your daily prompt.

Give yourself as much time as you need to master this synthesizing technique. Don't be in a hurry to rush through it or to move ahead to the culminating step. Always use a relaxation technique to begin the session, and always end with an affirmation.

Remember that this exercise relates only to those activities and events that you identify as most important during your day. There's an old axiom in traditional time management that still holds true for New Time: *If you do what is most important, you will have accomplished most of what you need to do in a day.* The difference in New Time versus old, of course, is that with Inner Time *you* decide what's important for you to accomplish and when to do it, rather than run on everyone else's clock.

The morning and evening visualizations are slightly different for this final step. In the morning you "rehearse" your day. In the evening you use the session to plan for tomorrow.

MORNING PROGRAM

1. Choose your favorite relaxation technique. Relax.

2. Visualize yourself standing before a closed door. Open that door and enter the first room. You are now in a room where you create intentional timeless nows. Select an intentional now for today. Experience it fully. What feelings do you have as you see yourself immersed in that intentional now? Enjoy the sensation of timelessness.

3. When you're ready, leave that room and open the next door. You are in the room of natural balance. See yourself in perfect balance in this room. Use all your senses to create this image. Go through your day in this balanced state. How do you feel? Notice how you are relating to others and how they relate to you.

4. Leave that room and open the next door. This is the room of purpose—where you make purposeful priorities part of your general day's plan. See yourself involved in purposeful priorities. What are they? Notice the emotions you are experiencing as you live on purpose.

5. Leave that room and open the next door. Enter the room of conscious choice. Feel the power that radiates in this space. Choose two situations in which you are successfully using the yes/no technique today. What are they? Quiet your mind and let the answers surface. Notice how you feel after having made these decisions.

6. Open the last door. Enter your "beautiful place." Perhaps it's a blooming garden or a quiet glade. Observe it closely. Notice any sounds that you hear, any sensations you feel. Pay attention to the colors and the aromas you experience there.

From this beautiful vantage point, imagine that you have completed the plan for your day as you intended to. Ask yourself these self-centering questions: "Were the activities I did in line with who I am—my state of being? Were they what I chose to do? Did they allow me to accomplish what I choose to have?"

Stay here a moment. Listen to your answers. Feel fulfilled and satisfied. Enjoy this place.

7. Complete the exercise with this affirmation: "Today I allow myself to set my own pace and be true to that tempo as I accomplish my significant activities."

EVENING PROGRAM

The evening program is a variation of the morning exercise. Here you will use three self-centering questions you posed in the morning exercise as a further deceleration technique. This visualization gives you practice in thinking through an activity before you commit to it. Again, this exercise helps to reduce the unnecessary pressure of overscheduling.

1. Begin with a favorite relaxation technique. Choose any one you like. Relax.

2. Go directly to your "beautiful place." See it and feel it with all your senses.

3. Envision your general plan for tomorrow. See yourself writing down the activities you want to accomplish. As you write down each activity, before you commit to doing it, ask yourself these three self-centering questions:

"Does this support who I choose to be?"

"Is this something I choose to do?"

"Does this allow me to accomplish what I choose to have?"

Pay attention to the signals you receive as you pose these three questions. Listen to your inner voice. If you cannot answer "yes" to all three as you consider an activity, cross it off your list or delete it from your plan.

Filter each activity through the three questions before deciding whether or not to commit to it.

As you see yourself with your plan in hand, what feelings do you have about it? Do you feel positive? Energized? Confident? Unhurried?

4. End with this affirmation: "I am growing in my ability to trust what feels good and right."

5. After finishing this visualization, write down your definition of time on a sheet of paper. Your initial definition may be as straightforward as "Time to me is the passing of the minutes and hours" or as philosophical as "I view time as precious, not a pressure." Each day this week, continue to add your thoughts to this definition until you have expressed a relationship to time that feels right for you. One twenty-one-year-old, about to embark on her career, ultimately worked out the following: "My concept of time has changed dramatically over the years. I used to view it with a sense of frantic tension; however, now I see time in much more relative terms. To me, timelessness is the original state of the universe and time is a manmade concept to help put a truly incomprehensible idea—that of our existence—into some conceivable perspective. If I could change the way the world views and uses time, I would try to alleviate the sense of pressure it imposes. Terms like 'rat race' and 'rush hour' would not exist; living for the present rather than for a rainy day would be emphasized, and the pace of nature would be the standard."

No exercise is included for getting you unstuck in this final step of the deceleration program. By the time you are ready to combine the four steps, you shouldn't be getting stuck anymore! If you find, as you practice this final step, that you cannot enter or leave any one of the "rooms" easily or cannot picture your to-do list in the evening, go back to the specific visualization exercise that teaches that technique. Having difficulty entering or leaving any of these rooms indicates that you need to practice intentional nows, balance, purpose, or conscious choice. Practice that particular visualization until you feel totally comfortable with it. Then begin again to use the synthesizing exercise.

LOOKING DOWN THE ROAD

As you begin designing your day, you'll notice another subtle but significant difference. Long-range planning, in the traditional time-managed sense, is eliminated. That formal session where you sat down every six months and wrote out a plan to follow simply becomes unnecessary.

This can be explained both theoretically and practically. In the pure Taoist sense, because there is no moment other than the now, the concept of the future is meaningless. Therefore planning for the future is a futile exercise. If you truly trust the river, accepting that a pattern has been printed for your life, it's unnecessary and even counterproductive to make elaborate future-oriented plans.

Practically, while you may embrace this concept intellectually, you might have difficulty imagining yourself living month to month with that idea. It's one thing to say you trust the river; quite another to leave your future to "chance."

Happily, as you design your time, you'll realize that you *are* planning long-range, just not in the way to which you've been accustomed. By concentrating on the now, continually checking for purpose and direction, and making conscious choices, you constantly fine-tune and adjust the state of your present—which is, after all, the goal of long-range planning. Put another way, your aims and goals become clear to you every step of your daily way so you do not need to make long-range planning sessions part of this process.

Then, too, even the time required to think through a problem will change dramatically as you practice these Inner Time techniques. With your new tool of visualization, something that may have taken you three days to ponder over will now become clear to you in minutes!

DESIGNING TIME

During the day, when you are sitting in traffic, waiting for an appointment, or relaxing in a sauna or a spa, return to your "beautiful place" for a few moments. Enjoy the feelings that it recalls.

Each time you visit it, you are reinforcing the four steps to mastering Inner Time. This idyllic setting, free from clocks or other time-induced pressure, is a trigger to help you stay committed to Inner Time techniques. Going to this place frequently reminds you to focus on intentional nows, check your balance, include purposeful priorities in your plan, and make conscious choices.

Just as your beautiful place helps you focus on the principles of Inner Time, asking the three questions helps to keep you on course when commitments and obligations threaten to engulf you.

How does this work? Let's say that you are contemplating a day in which you are going to have to fire three people because of company budgetary constraints. As you contemplate what's facing you tomorrow, you are angry, frustrated, and sad.

As you visualize this to-do on your list that evening, you ask yourself the three questions.

"What do I choose to be?" You answer, "I choose to be responsible in my job even when I know that many decisions are painful for me to carry out."

"What do I choose to do?" You may reply truthfully, "I choose to demonstrate that I am dependable and reliable, especially in sensitive situations."

"What do I choose to have?" "I choose to have peace of

mind knowing that I have carefully considered all the options and am doing the right thing in this situation."

By posing the three questions, you understand that this difficult task does support your sense of being, doing, and having. This makes it easier for you to accept that you do have to break the news to your employees. True, the job won't be any easier for you, but you have come to terms with it. What's more, instead of spending the evening fighting this decision or worrying excessively about it, you now can devote some of your time to making phone calls to friends in related businesses so that perhaps you can present your people with some options other than just severance pay.

That's not to say that part of you still won't be upset. Your new approach to thinking about time won't make you saintly—only sensible.

Why is this approach so effective? The answer is Taoist in its essence. By asking these questions, you focus completely on you—on what you choose to be, do, and have. You effectively clear your mind of extraneous thoughts. In doing this, you allow clarity to replace confusion. Instead of assuming an outer-directed stance—"How can he or she or they do this to me?"—you turn the focus inward. Now you may ask: "Why am I faced with this situation at this particular time? What is it that I am here to learn?"

This shift in focus away from the external "them" and on to the internal "you" is what will make the greatest difference in how you view and respond to demands on your time.

As you ask these questions every morning and evening, you'll notice that many of the decisions you make about your day won't differ substantially from those you may have made without going through the exercise. But by posing these questions, you continually recenter yourself. Answering these questions not only helps you know *why* you are doing what you do, it also prompts you to reaffirm the essential sequence of being, doing, and having.

Here's how one woman used these techniques to redesign her time.

Ann is a suburban mother of three, a wife, and a lawyer. She used to drive carpools four times a day, specialize in personal injury law, volunteer on weekends at the zoo, teach Sunday school, and frequently entertain for her husband's business clients. Meticulously organized, Ann never felt caught up. She was constantly running. Then, one day, she went to the dentist complaining about her tender jaw. She was shocked when her dentist told her that if she could learn to relax, the soreness would disappear. Ann listened, but she was disappointed. She was hoping for medication—not a lecture on life habits.

Within a month, however, she noticed other problems. She was fatigued more. Headaches came more frequently and lasted longer. Then her stomach started bothering her. She went to see her family doctor who, after running several tests, told her that her main problem was her life-style. Ann's physician counseled her that she needed to make some significant and lasting changes—soon.

Having heard the message twice, Ann was convinced she had to examine her life. As she thought about her days and nights, she quickly concluded that time was her worst enemy. Everything she did was a race against the clock. Even when she was spending time with her family, it was always tightly structured according to everyone's schedules.

After such discussion with her husband and children and reading up on stress-related diseases, Ann determined to make a change. She realized that, at age thirty-eight, she was racing so fast that if she continued accelerating at this speed, she'd be exhausted by the time she reached her fortieth birthday. She was heading for burnout—professionally and personally.

Ann began by identifying what was really important to her. Health and family came first. Her profession was a close second. Using our Inner Time techniques, she committed to using the visualization program twice a day. Within seven weeks, when Ann had created her "beautiful place," her family noticed the difference. As Ann's attitude about the amount of time she had to accomplish things changed, so did she. Where she was tense and quick, now Ann—although still an intense personality—is more relaxed and at ease.

But she'd be the first to tell you that making the change hasn't been easy. Just as when she initially saw her dentist, hoping for a simple medication, when she began the Inner Time program she still was looking for a "quick fix." Ann sincerely believed that she could do it all—that all she had to do was run more efficiently and faster. She disliked the idea of giving up anything in her life because she equated that with failure.

However, as she began working with the concepts of Inner Time, Ann realized that she had allowed her life to center on external cues. She'd bought the time package. She had never even questioned the authority of the clock.

Ann made some painful decisions. Among them, she decided that she needed to spend less time on her profession, be more selective in how she spends time with her children, and, generally, respond less automatically to demands of others. She spoke to the law firm and negotiated a more reasonable work schedule, agreed to drive only one carpool instead of two each day, and after talking with her husband, she decided that although she enjoys cooking for company, they would use a caterer or entertain together more at restaurants.

The choices weren't easy. Going to a lesser work schedule meant not only a cut in income but, even more significant for Ann, a change in status at the firm. It was a major hassle to get someone else to take that second carpool, and entertaining out was definitely more costly. But Ann made these choices willingly and consciously.

As she began to get in touch with intentional timeless nows, she made a habit of designing highlights into her day free of any clock-directed pressures. She goes to a yoga class weekly and makes a point of reading to her children after dinner. She was completely surprised by what she found when she investigated her balance. Although she assumed that she was someone who liked a fast and furious pace, she learned that she also needed regular periods of calm and quiet to recenter. Without these hiatuses, she didn't function well in any part of her life. Working on purpose gave her a sense of confirmation about the time she devoted to her family and law practice. But it also uncovered some latent interests that she'd ignored for years. Now, for instance, instead of volunteering weekly at the zoo, she helps on special events only and takes piano lessons instead for her own pleasure. Finally, while she thought that she was cool and decisive, when she got serious about conscious choice, she admitted that much of her time was spent reacting to what she thought were others' expectations of her. She was amazed to realize that she could say "no" to a colleague needing help on a case or a friend asking her to give up a weekend to work at a charity golf event, and neither person thought the worse of her.

Ann wasn't happy about making these changes at first. It was painful for her to admit that she had to change her habits. She'd assumed that time was the problem. Instead, she discovered that time had been a convenient excuse for her. As long as *it* was the issue, she was exonerated. Once she began to see time as unlimited, she had to confront herself. She couldn't do it all. No one can.

Today Ann goes to her "beautiful place" at least twice a day to remind her to stay with Inner Time. While she still has twinges of regret when she sees another lawyer handling an especially fascinating case that she might have gotten had she been working at her old schedule, or has to tell her daughter that she can't drive her to that special dance rehearsal, she's satisfied with the pace and direction of her life and feels better than she has in years!

As Ann discovered, she had to make choices. "A lot of

people who want to refine their time sense want something for free," says Larry Dossey, M.D., a Dallas internist and author who has pioneered in treating patients for time-perception problems. "They want their symptoms to disappear, but they want to continue to do what they are doing and not pay any price. You really don't get something for nothing."

While it may not take a crisis like Ann's to make you take note of your behaviors and relationship with time, Dossey warns, "There has to be an experiential connection that shows a person that he is willing to make a change. A lot of people are like alcoholics. They have to hit rock bottom before they do anything."

As you work on this final step, remember that the purpose of this deceleration program is to change your *attitude* about time. Only after you change how you perceive time can you alter its reality. At some point you may create your own visualizations, employ biofeedback, or use any of the many forms of meditation to establish inner awareness.

A marketing professional specializing in sports events admits that she changed her approach to time out of sheer frustration. "I never got everything accomplished. I never enjoyed what I was doing because I seemed never to be doing what I wanted when I really wanted to do it. I was always 'shoulding' myself. It slowly dawned on me that I was too achievement oriented and wasn't allowing time for my creativity to surface even though I was in a 'creative job.' Then I got married and discovered that I had to become more flexible, for now I had to take into consideration the schedules and preferences of a husband and two children."

After learning the Inner Time techniques, she developed her own version of the program. "What I do is begin each day visualizing my perfect day and seeing myself completing each major task successfully. Then it's like a Higher Sense of order steps in and shuffles what I will do—and when."

Larry Dossey's search for how best to relate to time has

taken him beyond visual imagery. His clinic teaches biofeed-back to help people readjust their perception of time, but Dossey doesn't personally practice that technique anymore. "I meditate when I know I need to, maybe several times a week. I sit on a couple of pillows to do this. What works for me is not specific imagery. I am attracted to emptiness. If a thought comes, I let it come, but then I let it pass away. I strive for a 'blank sheet of paper.' Other people use mantras or mandalas or chanting. I tried them, but this, the school of Vipassana meditation, suits me.

"Through the years I've learned that if you meditate enough, it becomes part of you. Then you can be relaxed and in a meditative state at the same time that you are going about your life. In the beginning, however, when you are first learning, I feel that a dedicated, disciplined schedule is very important to learning a technique."

"I know what works for me," says Deborah Madison, founding chef of The Greens restaurant in San Francisco and nationally known cookbook author. "I get up in the morning and have my coffee and am quiet for a half hour or so. I make my list of what I want to do that day. Then I put it away and don't look at it again until that evening or the next morning when I review it.

"During the day, I make notes to myself why things don't happen as I'd intended them to. Then once a week I sit down with two friends and we review our week together. We talk about why we are not getting our goals accomplished. It helps you to do this with friends because you articulate what's going on and you get to see your own patterns. We'll ask each other about the plans we'd each made, whether we got that as-signment completed or that project done. Talking about work-related problems often helps us see the larger issues. For example, if you find that you never seem to get things done in the early afternoon, you can tell that this time of the day isn't good for you. Maybe you should use that time to garden instead."

Madison concludes that reviewing their week together is a meaningful way for her to spend time with her close friends.

DEFINING TIME

Sometimes even a simple event can cause you suddenly to change your perception of time.

"I remember exactly when that happened to me," says Samuel Bleeker, a technology consultant from Gainesville, Florida. "I was in my early thirties and I was planting in my garden, something that I love to do. And I said to myself, 'I like this a lot.' I realized as I said it that I might only have maybe forty more plantings in my life. At once, I comprehended that life is limited. This experience was one of my trigger insights into time."

What followed, Bleeker says, was an awakening to an existential clock that is not unlike the ticking of the biological clock women in their thirties report hearing, "I wasn't as concerned with existential time when I was young," he says. "But in my thirties, this clock began ticking louder."

Today Bleeker runs on three different clocks. "I measure my existential clock by my own standards. This is an intensely personal time. This is the clock from which I create my own timetable for living. This clock tells me I may not make it to seventy, so I must write my book now. For me, this is the most fundamental clock."

At the same time, Bleeker also recognizes what he calls "other-directed" time. This is Interactive Time; it's the way one adjust one's own clock to others. For instance, if Bleeker knows that he has an appointment with a friend who is always late, he slows down. However, if he's to meet a friend who is punctual, his own sense of urgency is heightened.

The third clock, Common Shared Experience Time, "... tells me that it's nine o'clock or Thursday. This is where I am conscious of the flow of time as perceptible."

Bleeker says that he is conscious of all three clocks and can actually feel himself slipping from one mode into the next.

By removing yourself from the traditional, clock-driven way of thinking about time, you'll free yourself to begin to see time as it is for you. Many people say that this is the point at which they begin to see time as changing from being an enemy to being an ally. By establishing a friendship with time, you personalize it. You create a relationship that can grow and change. Because you are no longer threatened by time, you view it without fear or suspicion. From this perspective, you know that time works *with* you, not against you.

Here are how some other people define their time.

A therapist specializing in family counseling and death and dying offers this: "I feel that there is this web of time—a continuum that connects events. So if I end up with time I didn't expect to have—like missing a plane and being here for a few hours or a day—I use it to smell the roses."

"Time is a rhythm for me that keeps me in touch with who I am," says Michael Ray. "I used to view it as a commodity, always in terms of too little or too much. In the early 1970s, I gave up the fight and began to view time as an ally, and it was then that I began to live in the present."

"I know what time isn't," says Larry Dossey. "I know that time is not an entity. It doesn't flow from the past to the present to the future. Time isn't a thing. Those are old Newtonian ideas that have been summarily transcended by modern physics. I regard time as a product of consciousness."

"My definition of time has changed and altered," says a high school history and government teacher. "Over time, I've gone from the childlike stage of daytime and nighttime to being on time, being out of time, being a slave to time, and time being relative. There are even periods when my mind entertains the concept of no time."

A retired chairman of the department of Oriental studies of a large Western university writes: "Time is an abstraction.

So there really is no such thing as time. I think of living and flowing through transitions between events, not through punctuations in time. That way the Tao permeates *in spite of time*."

PAUSE FOR REFLECTION

1. You've created your "beautiful place" by walking through the four steps, and you can check your decisions concerning time by asking the three self-centering questions that explore being, doing, and having.
2. You've begun to define your personal relationship to time.
3. You now know that the four steps and the three questions are all you need to decelerate.

SECTION III

The Daily Way:
Old Time Tactics and
New Time Challenges

10

Getting Specific

There is no need to run outside
for better seeing.
Nor to peer from a window. Rather abide
at the center of your being;
For the more you leave it, the less you learn.

Lao-tzu

The deceleration program in the last section is aimed at helping you change your attitude about time. It starts you on a journey that will unfold as long as you remain committed to the concept. It gives you a "strategy" for organizing and managing your life.

But sometimes even the most dedicated attitude isn't enough to cope with daily time challenges. It's the little things that trip us up—deadlines, mail, meetings, interruptions, appointments. Faced with a barrage of time problems—without even realizing how or when it happens—we can slip back into our old time ways. As one frustrated executive put it, "I can handle priorities one through four okay. It's five to infinity that get to me!"

The "tactical" exercises described in the next chapters are designed especially to deal with specific time-related problems. They provide you with additional ammunition to cope with daily time crunches and to keep you focused on Inner Time when you may be tempted to fall back on your old ways. Think of these techniques as reinforcement to help you stay on track with the four steps of the deceleration program whenever you find yourself surrounded by chaos. Just as the deceleration exercises are aimed at helping you change your attitude about time, these tactical techniques help you keep committed to Inner Time all day long—regardless of the extent or amount of outside pressures.

You won't need to set aside fifteen minutes morning and evening to practice these techniques. Unlike the Inner Time program, these exercises are meant to be done on the spot. Common time problems you face each day usually demand instant attention. They need to be resolved at that moment— not contemplated after the fact.

The exercises have another benefit. Besides providing you with a measure of instant relief, each time you confront and resolve a specific time problem without falling back onto your old time habits, you'll be reaffirming and thus strengthening your Inner Time muscles.

At the start of each chapter, each time dilemma is first connected to one or more of the four steps of the deceleration program. This link with the four steps is vital because it ties each time problem to its underlying cause. For example, by confirming the connection between procrastination and pur- pose (chapter 7), the tactical exercise prompts you to look beyond your immediate predicament and begin, instead, to question why you are putting off taking action.

This section is easy reading. First, the old way of handling each time problem is described. As you read through these scenarios, you may see yourself in some of the old time man- agement techniques. If you do, that's great. Seeing yourself described in the old way of time may help clarify your current approach to solving that problem—an approach that's *not* working for you.

Next, the real facts of that situation are presented—what can be called the rest of the story. Here you can begin to see why you aren't completely comfortable with your present approach, why you are still running into trouble despite your best intentions.

In the "new way" section, you're given an Inner Time

method to substitute for your old, familiar technique. The mind game or exercise will help you resolve the immediate time crisis you're facing and, at the same time, keep you focused on Inner Time thinking so that you continue practicing what you've learned in the deceleration program.

As with the four decelerating steps, each of these New Time tactics ends with an affirmation. Affirmations not only help you "fix" your resolve, they act as firm reminders to keep you on track. Feel free to repeat these affirmations as often as you like during the day.

Under the final heading, "New Time in Action," you'll find additional practical suggestions pertaining to that specific time issue and examples of how other people who are successfully moving from outer to Inner Time are dealing with the same pressure. Their experiences may spark some idea of your own to handle these or other time problems you face.

Unlike traditional time-managed quick fixes, the tactical techniques presented in these chapters don't pretend to provide the absolute answers to time dilemmas. Only you can come up with those. These mind games, visualizations, and deep-breathing exercises are all designed with one purpose— to help you stay connected to your inner power when you're tempted to pull the plug. It may help you to use this section if you think of it as a bridge to move from outer to Inner Time. In effect, these exercises provide yet another way for you to connect with Inner Time. Each step that you take helps to move you along in your journey.

As you read over this section, don't try to memorize any of the exercises. Simply be sensitive to the problems and situations described and make a mental note of the ones that sound like you. Then, whenever you run up against one or more of them, go back to that chapter and use the technique that's designed to help you over a particular rough spot.

These techniques are not complicated or time-consuming. You can do them quietly and without calling attention to yourself. As Inner Time thinking becomes a habit, you may even start to devise your own exercises—images, mental games, even mantras that trigger the response you desire.

Once you learn how to trigger your desired response, you can apply that same method of problem solving to other aspects of your life. While this book is aimed at helping you find a new way of time, what you are learning has wide application.

THREE PRINCIPLES OF NEW TIME THINKING

All of the concepts presented in both the deceleration program and this tactical section are based on three fundamental principles. These principles may be applied to many different kinds of situations. Consequently, while the visualizations you invent may be quite different for each situation, your basic approach to problem solving won't vary.

To activate New Time thinking when you are faced with a dilemma:

• Begin by removing any existing barriers. Shut out the external world. Usually this means that you'll need to absent yourself from noise and traffic so that you can physically experience quiet. Quiet is a valuable asset, one that we are only now beginning to appreciate. Recent research indicates that not only does the absence of noise promote reflection and aid in strategic decision making, it also can be a powerful instrument for change.

• Creatively visualize the outcome or solution to a problem you are faced with. Visualize what you wish to happen. You can do this in any number of ways—through inventing mind games, deep breathing, or through visualization or meditation, to name just a few. Let your imagination run free as you picture or sense that desired outcome. Call up this image frequently.

• Having set the stage, listen for the answer you seek. Allow yourself to hear your inner voice.

Now, let's get on with how to deal with some of those more common time pressures. But before we do, remember—relax. Take a few deep breaths before you begin each exercise. Relaxation is always the first step.

11

Scheduling

CONNECTION:
Now moments

Old Way:

In a clock-driven world, the object of scheduling is to fit all our activities into an eight- or ten- or even fourteen-hour period. To move this process along, we are encouraged to use a time organizer, which is divided into days and hours. Our job becomes assigning activities to the appropriate time frames. In traditional time thinking, the focus is on predetermined scheduling—making sure that each activity is pinned to an appropriate block of time.

Fact:

As we think about our day, sometimes we feel overwhelmed by all that we have to do. In such instances, it's easy to fall back on scheduling as the answer to our problem. When we find ourselves starting to slip into the schedule-it-all trap, we must interrupt that behavior. Instead of overscheduling, we should reconnect to our intentional timeless nows.

New Way:

Begin by calming yourself. It is early morning and you see yourself sitting next to a waterfall. You are surrounded by huge rocks. It's shady here with just flickers of sunlight peeking through the rocks. As you sit beside the waterfall, feel the sunlight on your face.

In this comfortable setting, think about what you would like to accomplish today. Allow the waterfall to wash away your "shoulds" and "must dos." As you listen to the powerful surge of the water and feel the moist droplets of spray on your skin, sense the routine of your day slip away.

Refreshed and renewed, let the highlights of your day appear at the top of the waterfall. As these become clear to you, allow each highlight to tumble over the rocks, mixing with the flowing water. As each timeless now emerges and falls, feel yourself relax. Now allow the power of the waterfall to carry the remainder of items you choose to do today along as well.

Take a deep breath. Exhale slowly. Notice how good it feels to have identified your highlights. Notice how the other, less critical activities you choose to do today follow naturally once your highlights are clear. Take a second deep breath. Exhale slowly. Leave this setting and return to planning your day.

Affirm:

I deserve wonderful things to happen in my life today.

New Time in Action:

At the Dallas Diagnostic Association, patients suffering from "time sickness"—defined as a chronic sense of fighting the clock—are put to a simple test. They are asked to relax, close their eyes, and simply feel when one minute has elapsed. Dr. Larry Dossey, who helped found the clinic, reports that everyone drastically underestimates the deadline. The average "minute" experienced by patients is only thirty seconds; the record is five seconds.

This exercise illustrates that our chronic sense of fighting the clock has squeezed our perception of time until we don't have a real sense of it anymore.

Surely our own warped sense of time is partly to blame for our hurried state. If we can't judge a single minute accurately, how can we expect to know what we can reasonably expect to accomplish in an entire day?

To resist that urge to compress time, indulge in daily rituals. French author Jean-Louis Servan-Schreiber, writing in *The Art of Time*, notes that he makes "an appointment with time" each morning before breakfast. He uses this quiet time to plan his day on a sheet of paper and then, he writes, "I live it mentally." Other people find an early-morning walk or a before-work gardening session a way to establish their natural pace so that they stay in sync with real time. When you are synchronized with real time, you are less inclined to feel an urge to overschedule.

12

Finding Order and Sequence

CONNECTION:
Balance

Old Way:

Traditional time management teaches us to decide on our priorities by using an A, B, C system. After rating our to-dos, we categorize these priorities by assigning a number to each. For example, we may have three A priorities and five Bs. We break the As into A-1, A-2, and A-3, and so on. Then we complete the exercise by fitting each lettered and numbered priority into an appropriate slot of time.

Fact:

The busier we are and the more demands we experience on our time, the more order and sequencing can be a problem for us. Should we start to fear that we are losing control of our day—worrying excessively when and how we are going to get everything done—it's a sign that we need to check our balance. Although we may think that order is the problem, it isn't. What's happening is that our sense of balance and rhythms are out of sync. When we are comfortable with our inner balance, when the pace of our activities is in step with our natural rhythms, we move naturally from event to event and activity to activity powered by our sense of fun.

New Way:

If you suspect that you are falling back on your old time habits, selecting priorities mechanically or packing your schedule beyond what's comfortable for you to sustain, try this visualization. Because we usually consider order and sequence as we plan our day, practice this technique in the morning or in the evening as you think about how to organize your schedule.

See yourself awakening from a peaceful sleep. As you wake up, you notice a gold box sitting beside your bed. Curious, you open the box and find a note inside. In giant letters the message reads: TODAY YOUR ONLY MISSION IS TO HAVE FUN. KEEP YOUR IMAGE OF BALANCE PULSATING WITHIN AND AROUND YOU!

Quickly rethink your priorities for the day. If any priority doesn't connect with your sense of balance—if it doesn't measure up on the fun factor scale—drop it for today. Use the same image to check the order of events—how you intend to accomplish what you've planned.

If you are still worried about order and sequence, try this simple visualization. See each highlight of your day written on a separate sheet of paper. Just for fun, toss the sheets into the air. Watch as the papers slowly drift down to the ground. Pick them up. As you read them in their new order, be mindful of your mission. Shuffle your priorities in this manner until you feel satisfied and content with the arrangement of your day.

Affirm:

Nothing can stop me from feeling wonderful today!

New Time in Action:

Most people who are committed to deceleration ultimately develop their own pet methods to keep track of order and sequence. Doug Greene depends on his calendar, which he calls "my hard copy of my memory." Greene says he doesn't like to memorize anything, so he puts it down in his appointment book. "At the end of the day, everything in my calendar gets done or forwarded. Yet I don't feel tied to this book," Greene says. "I feel *connected* to it."

Terry Dalton, CEO and chairman of the board of The Unicorn Slept Here, Florida's largest and most successful natural life-style shopping center, runs his life and his $8 million company by jotting his agenda on a 5 x 8 yellow pad. "I use the small pad to keep track of things I plan to do that day," says Dalton. "I also keep a yellow legal pad, divided into four different columns that correspond to the departments at the Unicorn Village (the name of the natural foods shopping center in Miami). Whenever I have a thought that pertains to one of the departments, I write it down. Then when I meet with my operations directors, I work from that legal-size pad. I use my brain only for the intuitive process. I don't use it for memory at all."

Still another deceleration idea is to jot your to-do list on file cards—one item per card. Then have fun with your agenda by rearranging the stack of cards several different ways until you devise a plan of each action that *feels* right to you. Making the planning of each day into a game especially appeals to people who like the challenge of solving puzzles.

13

Procrastination

CONNECTION:
Purpose

Old Way:
> Traditional advice goes like this. If we tend to procrastinate, we should set short-term goals and reward ourselves for each step we accomplish as we head toward our ultimate goal. We confront our tendency to put off certain activities by taking the items we are most likely to leave for last, and plan to do these first. We save the other items—the ones we'll find easier to accomplish—for later in the day, and reward ourselves each time we manage to complete a task early in the day (that is, a task that we normally would have procrastinated about).

Fact:
> Often we procrastinate because we aren't aware how an activity or event suits our purpose or furthers our direction. It's easy to put things off when we don't have any desire to get them done. In the new way, procrastination acts as a warning signal to help us stay on purpose. If we notice that we are putting off an activity, it's a clear sign that our intended action is not supporting our direction.

New Way:
> Whenever you sense that you are starting to procrastinate,

get back on the purposeful track by playing the Detour Mind Game.

See yourself feeling happy and full of energy, ready to start your day. You are living on purpose and it's changing the way you respond to demands on your time. You are reorganizing your activities with a greater sense of self-accomplishment.

Visualize getting into your car at home to drive to an early-morning appointment. It's a meeting you are vitally interested in attending. Perhaps you are meeting with a new supplier who will save the company money and therefore reflect well on your record. You discover that your car won't start. What do you do? Solve this first detour in your plans.

Having arrived at your appointment, you find that the person you're to see is ill today. His office left a message with your office to that effect but you never received it. What do you do? Solve this second detour in your planned day.

On the way back to your office to attend a regular staff meeting, you run into a huge traffic jam, and by the time you arrive, the meeting has already adjourned. The numbers you were going to present were terrific and certain to earn you points with your boss. What do you do? Solve this third detour.

The object of this exercise is that you must solve each detour on the spot. You can dream up any situation or challenges for the game. The only rule is that you can't put off solving any detour. By forcing yourself to confront each difficult situation as it occurs, you actively work at overcoming your tendency to procrastinate. If the circumstances of this game don't fit your professional situation, make up one that does.

Notice that in this game, each situation is clearly tied to your purpose. You *want* to make that appointment and you *look forward* to the meeting because these activities support the direction you are moving in. Purposeful connection is the catalyst to help you shift out of "neutral" when you're tempted to stall.

Affirm:

Today I have the courage to look without fear at what needs to be changed to keep me on purpose.

New Time in Action:

Pay attention to the signals you give yourself. Be on the alert for procrastination when: you have what seems like an overwhelming project to do and you have trouble getting started . . . you're faced with a boring task and there's not much you can do to change it . . . you have an assignment that requires constant attention on your part . . . you're involved in a project or an activity where you won't see any immediate results . . . you just can't seem to summon that last big push to finish a job . . . you start cleaning everything else up first . . . just thinking about that activity makes you feel unusually tired . . . you hear yourself saying "I can't," "not now," or "later" more than you normally say these phrases . . .

In each of these instances, check for purpose. Each of these can be a warning signal of potential procrastination problems. Your best weapon against this is purposeful connection. Whenever you can identify how and where purpose is part of an activity, you are less apt to put off starting or completing a job. If you cannot find a purposeful connection after searching for meaning or direction, you may need to reconsider accepting or completing the task.

14

Overload

CONNECTION:
Nows, balance, purpose,
and conscious choice

Old Way:

When we are faced with many situations—all of which we perceive as needing to be handled at once—traditional time management urges that we seek some logical order before beginning to tackle these demands. Such order seems to follow from the most critical to the least critical priority. Perceiving that these all need to be done now, we turn to the clock to help us create some semblance of order.

Fact:

The message we receive is "too many things to do and not enough time to do them."

New Way:

Use the Inner Time technique of the three self-centering questions (page 152) before you commit to any activity. Answering the questions reduces the urgency of simultaneous nows and helps you establish a natural sense of timing.

During days when you still feel the mounting pressure of simultaneous nows, try this simple Clock Release. Close your eyes. Visualize a round white clock face. As you concentrate on the clock, position the numbers 12, 6, 3, and 9. Fix the minute and hour hands at 12. Slowly run the hands counterclockwise. Allow your eyes to follow the motion. Erase the numbers on the clock.

Free of the pressure of time, allow the natural order of events to emerge. Focus on a single task. Do it. Move on to the next. Continue until you have completed all your "nows."

Affirm:

Today I trust that I will know the right answers at the right time.

New Time in Action:

As Stephanie ran out of her office, she automatically checked her watch. She had an hour in which to run several important errands. She promised to meet her husband at the costume shop to pick out their outfits for the masquerade party. She needed to pick up a newsletter at the quick printers, cash her check at the bank, and stop at the grocery to shop for supper. She also hoped she could pick up a pair of hose at the department store, and if she had any extra time, she had phone calls to return.

Stopping first at the bank, the line at the drive-in window threw off her schedule by an extra ten minutes. Upset for cutting the hour so close, she sped on to meet her husband. When she arrived, breathless, he was already browsing through the racks. Tense and nervous that she wouldn't get through her lunchtime list, Stephanie's creativity vanished. All the costumes looked alike; she didn't have a clue which to pick.

Stephanie took a deep breath, and then another . . . and did the erase-the-clock visualization. Without the pressure of the clock, she concentrated on her now, *this* now. She looked through the costumes again. She got some ideas. As she and her husband began to put their costumes together, he commented that she seemed so relaxed and at ease, in contrast with her tense manner when she arrived.

Moving quickly from errand to errand, she accomplished most of what she wanted to do in that hour. She decided to go to the grocery after work. Without the pressure of the clock, Stephanie gained the clarity to see her way through the maze of immediate time demands.

15

Setting Goals

CONNECTION:
Purpose and conscious choice

Old Way:

We are taught to set long-term and short-term goals by looking at the various compartments of our lives. For example, we are encouraged to identify intellectual goals, physical goals, professional and social goals. Then we plan a strategy to achieve our aims and incorporate strategic steps as part of our daily activities. Having taken action, we monitor our results.

Fact:

Unless we feel personally conected to a goal, good intentions don't turn into actions. Connection gives us the energy to accomplish our aims. Conscious choice helps us activate that energy. Having made a conscious decision to take action, we're most successful when we begin from a state of being—when we start by "seeing" the goal as already having been attained.

New Way:

Whenever you identify a goal, make sure it supports your purpose. Then activate the power of conscious choice to move from dream to reality.

To practice this technique, choose something that you would like to improve about yourself. Perhaps you want to change a work habit. Maybe you want to cultivate a relationship, accrue more money, or concentrate on an issue that relates to your personal growth.

Whatever your goal, check it against your purpose. Does it support your direction?

Having established that connection, use the yes/no technique (page 133) to decide if you will take any action. If yes, identify when you will act.

Having decided that the time is right for you to start accomplishing your goal, see yourself having achieved it. Begin with the state of being. Ask yourself what you did to accomplish this goal. What are you feeling? What is different about you now that you have accomplished it?

Each time you think of this goal (and try to recall it once a day), run through the being scenario. Plugging into this state of being gives your goal power.

Affirm:

Today I am open to take a step forward in a new direction.

New Time in Action:

Sales expert Larry Wilson insists that the quality of his present is directly related to what he sees as the outcome of his actions. Goal-driven, he describes himself as having two speeds: stop and go. "When I stop, I use this time as an opportunity to reflect," says the dynamic entrepreneur. "Frankly, I'll always be high energy—with balance. I thrive on it."

To stay on purpose, Wilson explains that he thinks about time in relation to the goal—not to the clock. "I operate on goal time. I don't live with much sense of the clock. For instance, I don't break my life into time increments. Still, our company has done something that most people said was impossible to do and in a time frame that people said was totally impossible to meet. We've created a business that didn't exist three years ago, built from scratch."

Eric Utne, publisher and editor of the highly successful *Utne Reader* based in Minneapolis, admits that he originally intended the magazine to be a newsletter done out of "my hip pocket." "But when it was evident that it was going to take off, I took the leap and turned it into a full-fledged bimonthly publication. Being in print was my first goal. My second goal was that the magazine would be a part of my life and not my whole life. Today, when people ask how the magazine is doing, I find that I answer, 'We work regular hours.' For me, that's a measure of success."

Utne begins any new project or idea from an intense state of being. "When I have a sense of something happening, I see it very clearly," he says. "For me, that image is so real that I'm frustrated that others can't see my vision. I'm told that because of this—my seeing something as if it's already happening—that when I'm trying to persuade others to a new idea, it sounds like I've already made a decision when in fact I haven't. I've had to learn that there's a process to bringing an idea into reality that must include other people."

16

Interruptions

CONNECTION:
Although all four concepts are involved,
handling interruptions in a way that
is comfortable for you
and gives you results is an indication that
you are in balance.

Old Way:

Interruptions are time-wasters and, as such, deserve combative strategies. Traditional solutions are found in external messages—shutting the office door, using a secretary as an interceptor, adopting certain body language, writing memos instead of having conversations, or employing various techniques to streamline meetings. The underlying message is clear: If we can immunize ourselves against unwanted interruptions, we'll be more productive and successful.

Fact:

Interruptions aren't necessarily all bad. Spontaneity can bring happy surprises. The trouble with most interruptions is not with the interrupter—it's with us. Interruptions stop our flow of thought and action. When we're distracted, our energy dissipates and we're less effective.

New Way:

Instead of seeing interruptions as interference, envision them as potential connections. Then make a conscious choice whether or not to connect.

Balance is your best indicator when deciding whether

or not to accept an interruption. You already have your perfect image of balance. Bring it up frequently on days when you feel especially fragmented. You'll find that focusing on your balance symbol can quickly help you recenter when interruptions throw you off.

Should you be overwhelmed by interruptions, try this Symbolic Balance Meditation.

The *I Ching* uses many symbols of nature in the belief that nature is itself the most accessible teacher of our awareness. One of these symbols, the mountain, signifies power and endurance. These qualities suggest centeredness.

To regain centeredness, close your eyes. Feel the vast power of the mountain. Experience the strong, quiet patience of the rocky mass. Feel the strength that emanates within and around it. Slowly walk toward the mountain. Feel yourself become one with it. You may hear the mountain speaking to you. What does it say?

Recall this enhanced image of balance whenever you feel frustrated by excessive interference. Being the mountain gives you the power to refocus your scattered energy. Instead of allowing yourself to be distracted, the mountain image helps you become directed.

By recalling your image of balance and by being the mountain frequently, you'll project an image of centeredness that others will respond to. You'll be surprised to find that you'll be subject to fewer interruptions because other people will be aware of your directed attitude.

Affirm:

Today I know that I can handle any change, any surprise, anything at all.

New Time in Action:

Doug Greene meets interruptions head on. The publishing and health food executive says, "I approach time by being very available. I've found that most people respect my time. They really don't need me; they simply want to get something done. When they discover that they can accomplish what they want to without talking directly to me, they do."

Terry Dalton, on the other hand, manages interruptions by connecting with extreme caution. "I consciously unplug myself from the system," he says. "It's part of the reason for my success. Being disconnected allows me to react to the now moment. That's essential in business.

"I don't have a car phone," Dalton says. "I don't carry a beeper. I screen all calls. Some days I won't take any calls; other days I'll take a couple. I don't even have an answer phone at home. If I don't get the message, then I'm not obligated to return it. On the other hand, I have an associate, a CEO of a film company in Miami, who carries two car phones! He's like the White Rabbit, yet he's still tuned in to his intuitive side. He talks and runs and works eighteen hours a day."

"Interruptions bother me only if I am really under a deadline," says Pam Del Duca, a Scottsdale, Arizona, entrepreneur and president of the Del Star Group, a corporation she started and nurtured to encompass fourteen different retail operations. "I think the fragmentation of a day is what makes it interesting. I get upset when friends say that they did not stop by to see me because they thought I was busy. What fun is being successful if you must insulate yourself from experiences?"

17

Communication

CONNECTION:
Balance

Old Way:
Traditional time management often treats effective communication lightly. Yet faulty communication continues to cause major time problems. When we don't understand an assignment completely, for example, we may have to go back and start it over again. Time becomes the issue, and what could have been handled in twenty minutes becomes a two-day nightmare.

A few time management courses do touch on communication skills. They suggest that we plan our conversations in advance for scheduled meetings, phone calls, and appointments. Basically, these recommend that we keep a written record of all these important communications, where decisions are being made or important recommendations agreed upon. The suggested format is: I SAID, YOU SAID, which is designed to illustrate accountability.

Fact:
Communication continues to be one of the major problems involving time, if not *the* problem. Because each person speaks from and listens with his or her own filters of experience and emotion, even clearly stated opinions, ideas, or directions can be misconstrued. The most effective communication is simple and direct. To achieve this, we must have clarity before we speak or listen.

New Way:

Being in balance and at ease with the pace of our life positions us for effective communication. When you aren't harassed or anxious, you speak and listen more productively. Before you participate in an important conversation, check your balance and rhythms. Connect to Inner Time by shutting down the external noises and recentering with the following Laser Breathing Technique.

Find a place to sit quietly and practice circular breathing (pages 86–87) for one to two minutes. As you continue to breathe rhythmically, concentrate on your inhalation and exhalation. As you inhale, visualize that you see a laser beam of light in front of you. As you exhale, notice that this beam of light is pure and focused and that you can direct it anywhere you wish. Continue to breathe in and out, playing with the light until you achieve your state of balance.

Visualize the laser beam as your communication path— the route that enables you to cut through the extraneous clutter of your spoken and written conversations. Use the image of the laser to simplify and direct your thoughts and words.

Affirm:

Today I allow myself to speak directly and to listen openly.

New Time in Action:

"Communication is always a problem," admits Ben Cohen of Ben & Jerry's ice cream. "So I consciously work at it. I try to be clearer. I try to be less emotional. I try to repeat. I try to confirm. Most of all, I am a good listener."

As you begin slowing down and establish a comfortable work and social pace, you'll find that it's easier for you to be a good listener. Hearing what is actually being said is the key to effective conversation. Listening is nine-tenths of communication.

18

Meetings, Appointments, Deadlines

CONNECTION:
All four steps

Old Way:

Meetings, appointments, and deadlines are fixed points in time that we must accommodate. We often feel that we have little control over these situations.

To combat that feeling of helplessness when faced with an inordinate number of meetings or appointments or the pressure of a fast-approaching deadline, we're taught to divide these time blocks into "high demand–low demand" tasks. Or we can categorize them according to the payoff we receive from accomplishing them.

To expedite the doing of all these blocks of time, we're urged to compartmentalize these tasks in some way. Organizing these demands by category gives us a logical way to work through them.

Fact:

This approach, while reasonable, is a "quick fix." Although we may gain a feeling of control from compartmentalizing, the sensation doesn't last because we never deal with the real issue—how these activities complement our balance, advance our purpose, or further our state of being, doing, and having.

New Way:

When your Inner Time attitude is assaulted by too many activities and "to dos," and you find yourself beginning to react negatively to a day packed with meetings, appointments, or deadlines, try this Energy Visualization.

Relax. Focus on your breathing. Bring up an image of a black night sky. Notice how tense you feel as you scan that dark expanse. There's not a star showing through, not a sliver of moon visible.

Imagine each appointment, meeting, or deadline as a ball of bright, positive energy. Select any one of them. Place it in the night sky. Watch it explode. As it explodes, notice how any anxiety you have about that appointment, meeting, or deadline dissolves. Continue placing each ball of energy in the sky until you've arranged everything that is pressuring you. Light up the sky with the energy of these fixed points in time. As the eruptions fade in the night sky, feel your tensions vanish.

Affirm:

Today I will see the highlights of my day as energizing opportunities.

New Time in Action:

When Florida technology consultant Samuel Bleeker faces deadlines, he says he goes into "turbocharge." "Time gets compressed. There is no tomorrow. It's only now. In the last ten years I've learned how to let time expand—like a gas. Before I learned how to do this, I would always do a task right away. Now I let it expand to fill the time. And I never miss a deadline.

"For me, time is an internal pressure. The more involved I am in a project, the more I internalize the task and the less the issue of time invades. I measure time in different ways. For instance, I have a different intensity for work time than I do for leisure time. Ultimately, time becomes Taoist—an endless, flowing river."

Robert Schwartz, former assistant to the publisher of *Life* magazine and New York bureau chief for *Time*, is best known as a co-founder of an executive training center. Schwartz concedes that he used to be a time-and-motion freak. "But today," he admits, "my life is fairly messy. I am always fighting my own ineptitude with time. Deadlines are useful to me. In the deepest psychological sense, a deadline is an artful death, and nothing is as unsettling as that."

Still another view is offered by Barbara Marx Hubbard. "I turn deadlines into lifelines," she says.

Muses Eric Utne, "Sometimes I wonder whether I'm not a deadline junkie. We writers are geniuses at giving ourselves false deadlines and then sniffing out the 'real deadline.' We push ourselves to the limit. I wonder if I didn't get involved in publishing because I love the ebb and flow of the business, the rhythms of deadlines. Because we are a bimonthly, we have intense periods followed by easy times and then pick up again."

By focusing on the energy encompassed in appointments, meetings, or deadlines, you can use these fixed points in time to generate action. Many successful businesspeople make a habit, for instance, of announcing deadlines publicly at the outset of a new project, declaring that their time frame helps them mobilize to meet it. In *Winning, the Innovation Game*, Denis E. Waitley and Robert B. Tucker note that Thomas Edison called a press conference to announce his latest innovation whenever he came up with a new idea. Then he'd go back to the lab and invent the product!

19

Mail Mountains
and Other Molehills

CONNECTION:
Conscious choice

Old Way:
Mail and paperwork are best handled by establishing a filtering strategy that usually begins with a secretary and moves through a filing system. We label mail with code words such as "toss," "refer," "act," and "file" to facilitate the basic premise of traditional time management: Handle each piece of paper only once.

Fact:
More recently, the electronic office has increased not only the flow of mail but also the speed at which it is delivered. Although we may diligently filter, intercept, and file all this information, we still can feel inundated by the barrage of paper and electronic data.

New Way:
That traditional advice, "Handle a piece of paper only once," remains valid. However, with Inner Time, you use conscious choice to decide the fate of each piece of information. Whenever you find yourself feeling confused and frustrated as you sort through mounds of incoming mail, try this symbolic Fire and Mountain visualization.

Call upon the symbol of fire from the *I Ching*. Fire is

a symbol of transformation. Although it may be interpreted in many ways, for our purposes it tells us that we are clinging to something we need to release. By invoking the image of fire and letting it move and burn, transformation begins to take place.

Imagine your room filled with paper. See it stuffed with stacks of unopened mail, correspondence waiting to be completed, and articles demanding to be read. There is no furniture in this room—just four walls and mounds of paper that all pertain to you.

Enter this room and close the door. Close your eyes and imagine yourself as fire. Feel the heat you give off. Hear the sounds of fire starting to burn. Smell the scent of smoke. As you (fire) build in intensity, realize that you may choose what to burn and what to save.

Move swiftly through the room, burning only what you decide to destroy. When you have ignited all those papers, allow the fire to die out. Reflect on this experience. Were you able to move through the room easily and decisively? What does this tell you about your perceived need for information? Which papers did you choose to leave untouched?

Affirm:

Today my power is within me.

New Time in Action:

Gauge your data appetite and then set up an appropriate screening system that supports your making conscious choices. If you crave information—you don't like to miss out on anything and like to get your facts firsthand—you probably prefer to screen most of your own mail. Terry Dalton does this by standing as he sorts it, directing it to the appropriate department and tossing away what he doesn't need in a large wastebasket he puts next to him. Standing keeps him on his toes mentally. He can't get too comfortable, so he sorts through the stacks quickly.

If you prefer to control the stream of incoming data,

set up a chain of command that assures that you handle only key items—necessary correspondence, magazines, newspapers, and so on. Scott Alyn, for example, has his mail so carefully filtered that he doesn't even see catalogues or magazines he doesn't choose to see.

Once you set up your initial screening system, devise an organizing technique that works for you. Your system should help you stay clear and focused and remove the guilt you get from looking at stacks of unread paper. You don't want to avoid reading newspapers and magazines, you just want to read them when it's convenient. Here are some ideas that are proven winners:

• Go through magazines and tear out articles of interest. Discard the magazines and save the articles in a special folder to read later at your convenience.

• Take notes on index cards when you read useful articles and attach these cards to the published piece. Writing it down helps you keep your mind clear for creative work.

• Make files general enough to be easy to use, yet specific enough to give you a sense of direction. Many executives keep files labeled PEOPLE TO WATCH ... PRODUCTS TO FOLLOW ... FINANCE IDEAS ... PERSONAL GROWTH. Having files already labeled and waiting makes it easy to save and retrieve information when you want it.

• Use mail as a quick resource. Scan incoming mail for a sense of where popular culture is heading. Observe hair and clothing styles in fashion catalogues. Note trends in relationships and music that are revealed in the headlines of the popular press. You don't have to read everything to glean information.

• Clip and save catalogues for ideas just as you file magazine articles. If an item, presentation, or photograph strikes you, tear it out and save it. Heed those intuitive signals!

• Use any "help" that works to draw attention to key

ideas. Post-its are great! So are highlight pens. Or scribble a summary note in the margin.

• Recycle your mail to sharpen your focus. Get in the habit of jotting down brief replies on the letter you receive and sending that letter back instead of drafting a new piece of correspondence. Keep a copy of the letter with your reply for your files. You save energy—and paper.

• Continue the "Cliff Note" habit. Subscribe to and read newsletters and periodicals that summarize information you find interesting or pertinent.

If, after setting up a screening system that fits your needs, you continue feeling inundated by incoming mail—ending up each day with four overflowing baskets all marked for your IMMEDIATE ATTENTION—you may need to consider what these mounds of mail indicate about yourself and your need for information and control. Letting go may be the real issue here—not your fax, FedEx, phone, or incoming mail.

20

Delegating

CONNECTION:
Balance and conscious choice

Old Way:

We are often exhorted to do what we do best. Know our strengths and our weaknesses, the advice goes. Know our staff's strengths and weaknesses, as well. We use this information to make decisions when relegating tasks. We decide who is best able to handle a project or assignment and then delegate it to him or her.

Fact:

While the above advice is sound, real life is not always so clear cut. Problems arise not only in communicating the nature of an assignment, but in letting go of the responsibility. When we are uncertain whether or not we want to delegate an activity or project, our reservation may show up as poor communication, which can lead to even more problems. That's why we often end up rationalizing that it's better if we do a job ourselves.

New Way:

Knowing our balance and checking it against the fun factor helps us determine how much we can comfortably commit to do. Once we've decided what we can do and what will be fun to do, we call on conscious choice to help us make the decision. Employing conscious choice, we conclude whether or not we should take on a responsibility and, if so, when.

Despite your best intentions, sometimes you may find that the old habit of not wanting to let go reappears when you are in the midst of making a delegating decision. To move beyond this old pattern, try this Canyon Wall visualization.

You are standing at a lookout point poised over a steep, rocky abyss. You see the vastness of nature's work. You have a list of situations you wish to delegate. Each situation is written on a separate page of a pad. As you read the first aloud, you tear that page off the pad. Drop the page over the wall of the canyon. Breathe deeply as you watch the paper fall away, fluttering in the breeze. Continue reading and dropping each situation over the edge of the canyon, letting each fall away until you've completed your list. Walk away from the scene secure that you are ready to release your hold on the responsibilities that you wish to delegate.

Affirm:

Today I allow myself to let go easily.

New Time in Action:

Mo Siegel, co-founder of Celestial Seasonings Herbal Tea Company, has stated, "Never hire anyone unless he's smarter than you are in the area in which he's going to be working for you."

"I've learned a lot about delegating recently," says Pam Del Duca of the Del Star Group. One of the top three National Small Business Persons of the Year in 1986, Del Duca is known for her youth, entrepreneurial spirit, and civic commitment. "Within the last year we went from five retail stores—each a different shop—to fourteen, with more on the way. For example, we added four resort gallery shops, a woman's apparel shop, and a flower business. I had no choice but to learn to delegate because I couldn't grow my businesses unless I did!

"What helps me let go is to see myself as if I were on an airplane. From a distance, all problems look small. Nothing seems so threatening. From up here, I see everything very clearly and I know exactly what I need."

A classic "hands-on" manager, Del Duca recently made a significant move from being a blue-collar (or controlling) entrepreneur toward white-collar (or managing) status. "I hired an executive to take over all the buying for all my stores," she relates. "Before this person came on board, I worried that I couldn't let go of the buying and I worried about every scenario I could imagine. I 'catastrophized.' What changed everything was when I finally realized that I really love what I am doing, that creating stores is my long suit. When I admitted to myself that I am successful because I'm good at what I do, talented, and not just lucky or profitable in spite of myself, my attitude changed and it became easy for me to let go. By letting go of this responsibility, I've freed myself to be creative again. My ideas for stores are limitless. Of course then I start to worry that maybe we are too diversified a company. With so many different stores, it's that much more work. But then I relax and return to the fact that diversification is my strength."

21

Overcommitment

CONNECTION:
All four steps, but conscious choice
is the activator.

Old Way:

Time demands are hard to handle because they come from all directions, register at varying levels of urgency, and assume different degrees of importance.

To deal with overcommitment, we're taught to analyze how we use our time each day. We identify obstacles—such as having agreed to complete an activity that we should have eliminated—and patterns of behavior that contribute to the problem.

Fact:

Despite this sensible approach, overcommitment remains a frequent time complaint. Saying "no" is not a time problem, it's a personal challenge.

New Way:

Using conscious choice, you learn that saying "no" can be a positive and powerful technique. Should you start saying "yes" when you want to say "no," you may need to practice your negative response.

Use private moments—driving to work, running errands, or showering—to get in touch with how you sound and feel when you say "no." Imagine you are having a conversation with a friend who is asking you to do something that is inconvenient. Say "no" to your friend, and if necessary repeat the exercise, perhaps varying the way you say "no," until you can do so easily and without extensive explanations. Like saying "good-bye," saying "no" is best done briefly and directly.

Affirm:

Today I have the choice to say "no."

New Time in Action:

Negotiation is nothing more than saying "no" so you can ultimately say "yes." Here's how saying "no" can work for you.

• Buy time and space—Saying a qualified "no" gives you the opportunity to do additional research so you can reconsider or reaffirm your stance. Use the time to analyze why you are saying "no."

• Let the world turn—Say "no" for now and watch what develops. If you don't like a situation as presented, saying "no" at that moment can open the door for you to say "yes" when circumstances change.

• Make "yes" count—Turning down some requests gives you the time and energy to say "yes" to those meaningful time commitments that you always wish you had time for.

• Stay on course—When your instincts tell you to say "no," pay attention. Checking your direction often is a good way to stay on track. According to the Monitor Report, a recent public opinion and behavior survey conducted by Yankelovich, Clancy, and Shulman, a noted firm that charts public trends, people in the 1990s will discover that they don't need to be all things to everyone, but they do need to be what they say they are.

22

Adjusting to Others

CONNECTION:
Balance and purpose

Old Way:

We have accepted a time management system that rewards us for responding positively to others' time demands. Efficiency systems are designed to foster that ideal. That's why such systems have space for personal, professional, and social obligations. One goal of traditional time management is to become a "well-balanced person," which is defined as someone who sets aside time for all of these areas every day.

Fact:

While the goal of these systems—to help us cover all bases faster and more efficiently—is admirable, the result often is additional stress. That mythical "balanced" person can easily turn into an anxiety-ridden "superwoman" or a time-pressured "man in the fast lane." Instead of enjoying their accomplishments, superachievers, hooked on acceleration, may have difficulty identifying when they are "balanced enough."

New Way:

By incorporating purposeful priorities into your day, you

focus on your goals and direction. Because you continually check your state of balance, you recognize early on when another's agenda or pace does not complement your own. Consequently, although you respond to others' time cues, you are able to do so within the framework of your own pace and rhythms.

Because multiple and conflicting time demands can be difficult to handle, sometimes you may find yourself reacting negatively to others' demands on your time or feeling forced to maintain an uncomfortably fast pace. Should this happen, look inward for balance and direction and try this Up Against the Wall visualization.

Stand facing a wall. Using a real wall is best, although you may just visualize doing this. Put your palms on the wall and press against it. As you gently apply pressure, visualize the wall crumbling. As it disintegrates, allow your reactions and/or attitudes to crumble with the wall.

Having removed the wall, see your image of perfect balance hanging in space. Take that image and hold it in your hands. Feel yourself regain your equilibrium. Sense your direction. Physically clearing a space in this manner gives you emotional elbow room in which to maneuver. Instead of feeling inundated and at the mercy of others, you succeed in creating your own personal space.

Affirm:

Today I choose to treat everyone as I like to be treated.

New Time in Action:

Hattie Babbitt, an attorney and wife of former Arizona governor and Democratic presidential candidate Bruce Babbitt, states, "Bruce's strength is that he's merciless about doing what he wants to do—unlike many of us who end up doing other people's agendas." Noting that her husband is not distracted by any external stimulus, she says, "Bruce is not even aware if he's hot or cold or if it's noisy. This leaves him free to spend lots of energy on doing what he chooses to do. Of course his biggest strength is also a problem for me because you have to get used to living with a person like this. He's not aware that I am having a crisis unless I stand in front of him and do something dramatic."

After twenty years, this couple has developed a form of communication that is at once interpretive and direct. Hattie, for example, has relaxed her expectations about Bruce's sense of time. "If he says he's going to be home at six o'clock, I don't count on that. This is an easy step that's made life smoother, but it was a major adjustment for me because I began life with him twenty-three years ago as Ms. Punctuality. I'm sort of a Dudley Do-Right. I viewed it as rude not to show up when you said you would. Now I know that he never watches the clock and has no idea of the hours passing."

They both are sensitive to demanding time from each other. "When Bruce was governor we had a system for making time demands on each other," she says. "We used a code phrase: 'Command Performance.' If Bruce told me it was a 'Command Performance,' I went and stood and smiled—no questions asked. I could—and did—request the same of him. Of course the crux of this is that you can't abuse the system. He maybe used it six times a year.

"What's helped me understand his use of time is spending a day with him every so often either at the office or on the campaign trail. I see people pull at him, wanting to get a little piece of him, almost like a feeding frenzy. I understand that you have to be merciless about saying 'no' or you couldn't exist in the face of all those demands." Happily, she says he's equally ruthless about saying he is going to devote his time to his family, law practice, and those international events that are most important to him.

While we feel a mate's time cues keenly, we also sense pressures from business and professional contacts. Sometimes it's advantageous to make adjustments. During Bruce Babbitt's 1988 primary campaign, for instance, he deliberately modified his use of time. He consciously speeded up his reactions to accommodate the accelerated pace of the campaign. Although his natural instinct is to take his time, read through material uninterrupted, reflect and relax, he mastered the fine art of the instantaneous response. Babbitt was able to accelerate successfully for that period of time because this change supported his larger purpose. "The premium goes not to the candidate who is the most thoughtful, intelligent, and incisive," Babbitt said, "but to the one who is the quickest and most quotable."

To make conecting easier at home and at work, Pierre Mornell, M.D., author and psychiatrist, recomends that we consciously build "transition time" into our daily routine. "We need a transition between the intensity of our job and the intimacy of our relationships," he writes in *Thank God It's Monday, or How to Prevent Success From Ruining Your Marriage.* Transitions encourage you to finish one part of the day and prepare for the next, Mornell says. By deliberately shifting gears, you can climb off your fast track, whether it is a houseful of children or an officeful of appointments, and slow down gracefully. These pauses can be as simple as fifteen minutes to read the mail before getting the home report, or as structured as a planned workout at the gym. Transition time can help you live better with others' time cues.

23

Using Extra Time

CONNECTION:
All four steps

Old Way:

We are urged to fill unexpected extra moments by doing more tasks. For instance, we can catch up on reading while waiting for an appointment, return telephone calls from our car phone while we are stuck in traffic, balance our checkbook while standing in line to buy tickets to a concert, or receive faxes while we catnap.

Fact:

Although doing double and even triple time can be effective, we also need quiet moments for renewal. Quiet times allow us to sense our balance and rhythm. Rather than using waiting time to accelerate, we should learn to value these times for deceleration.

New Way:

When you are given unexpected "free time," say this to yourself to unplug from the clock. You: "Here I am waiting again. What would be fun to do?"

Sit quietly and listen for the answer. Then follow through on it, no matter how crazy it seems. Your inner voice might urge you to run around the block or get an ice-cream cone.

Or it may encourage you to concentrate on rhythmic breathing. Whatever it tells you to do, do it.

Enjoy this gift of time, free of guilt or "shoulds." See it for what it is—an unintentional timeless now. Be open to it and let it renew you.

Affirm:

Today I allow myself to have fun when I'm faced with a delay.

New Time in Action:

The best way to wait when you are not physically able to do something else is simply to use this time for "instant replays." One woman who spends much of her time in her car going to and from appointments uses waiting time to run her personal memory tapes of special experiences. "When I'm sitting in traffic, I'll recall a day when I was cross-country skiing and the sky was absolutely clear and the snow silvery white. Instead of getting upset at the delay, I enjoy this time because I transport myself to another "place." I actually enjoy the wait. When else would I have time to relive such a wonderful experience?" she says.

SECTION IV

The Way of Time

24

The Next Generation:
Teaching Your Children
about New Time

As you read and reflected on the four phases of the deceleration program—living in the now, going within for balance, living on purpose, and exercising conscious choice—you may have thought, "I looked at time like this when I was a child." You probably did. Preschool children have an intuitive understanding of time that closely parallels the thought process described by the philosophy behind our "Tao of Time." Children follow all four steps naturally. Very young children live in the now. They instinctively respect their rhythms. They inherently act out their purpose. And, as parents of preschoolers quickly learn, toddlers' choices almost always reflect their own needs!

It's only as youngsters are immersed in adult culture and conditioned to society's clocks that their approach to time changes. Watching grown-ups battle time—racing against the clock, dashing off to work, bemoaning their time crunches—children get the message. In the real world, time is an adversary. The world is a rushing place where time often is all that matters.

Parents remain the principal architects of a child's view of time. Unwittingly, we imbed our cadences in our children.

"We hurry our children because we hurry ourselves," observes David Elkind in *The Hurried Child: Growing Up Too Fast Too Soon.* "We are a time-oriented society, and as parents, we pass these values on to our children."

As children grow, they are introduced to more sophisticated time concepts. Up to about a year of age, infants show no sense of segmented time. By age two, they are using the term "today." By two and a half, children begin speaking of "tomorrow." By age three, the concept of "yesterday" emerges. Morning and afternoon are notions that come into play by age four, and by age five youngsters can count time in days.

With the onset of kindergarten, a child's concept of time undergoes subtle modifications. While time is still viewed as unlimited, school and the school schedule introduce the idea of boundaries. As young children progress in school, they are expected to handle increasingly complex time segments—periods for subjects, timed tests, overnight deadlines. All of these concepts refine a youngster's idea of time and also affect how children see themselves.

As children internalize these lessons about time, they begin to understand that time has control over them. Instead of the unlimited world of the very young child, school-age youngsters begin to view the universe as divided into segments, periods during which they are expected to perform in certain ways. With each advancing stage, a child's sense of time becomes increasingly sophisticated. Not that this comes naturally. Studies reveal that children resist coming into our time-ruled society. Nevertheless, by age sixteen most youngsters have made the switch.

PARENT-CHILD SYNCHRONICITY

Babies know their needs instinctively, but parents teach them to identify these needs with time. Because adults link time to specific occurrences, young children soon conclude that time is something concrete, as tangible as a page from a calendar. We never completely lose this concrete sense of reckoning. To some degree, time always remains synonymous with activity. When we recall a special moment from our childhood, for instance, we don't say that it occurred on a specific date. Rather, we pinpoint the experience by an event. We'll say that we broke an arm at camp, the summer that we'd just learned how to swim. Or we remember that we had this revelation about growing older while on a high-ride at an amusement park with our grandfather.

Tying time to events is just one way we synchronize our inside tempo to the many outside clocks. Synchrony is a universal trait that is recognized almost immediately at birth. At about six months after conception, when the myelination of the auditory nerve takes place, fetuses start to hear. Immediately after birth, not only will an infant move rhythmically to the mother's voice but he or she will also respond rhythmically to other people's voices—no matter what language is being spoken. Provided that we start early enough, when these patterns are being learned, it appears certain that normal human beings can synchronize with any human rhythm.

Our timing mechanism is so natural that we hardly notice it—except when it isn't there. T. Berry Brazelton, a Boston pediatrician who has spent his career exploring parent-child interactions, states that a subtle, multilevel synchrony is present in normal parent-child relationships. Parents who batter their children, Brazelton suggests, have never learned to synchronize with their babies.

Parents who are changing their approach to time should question how their youngsters perceive and experience the world. Questioning parents should ask:

Am I in sync with my children?
Do I expect them to comply with my concept of time?

If I'm feeling frustrated with my present use of time, are my children mirroring my feelings?

Stress results when children's coping limits cannot keep up with adult schedules, when demands for adaptation surpass a child's energy supply. Stress is no longer an adults-only domain. Many young children are experiencing grown-up problems. Where once only children of elementary school age and older were heavily scheduled, now it's common for pre-school children to be intensely programmed. Parents push. Teachers insist. Coaches demand. And children comply as best they can.

NEW TIME FROM TODDLERS THROUGH TEENS

Since babies and toddlers absorb what's happening in their environment, parents who rush through the day in a perpetual state of panic or confusion should stop hurrying long enough to consider the time model they're presenting to their young children. If you fight time constantly, more than likely your child will copy your actions. If, on the other hand, you're at ease with time, your child will reflect your calm.

Early childhood is an ideal period to instill the basics for a new approach to time, since most of a child's learning takes place during the first five years of life. Small children are primed for New Time because their intuitive brain functions freely. To teach New Time to your children, make the concepts presented in chapters 5–8 part of their daily lives. These concepts come naturally to the young.

As parents of very young children know, children naturally live in the now. If they want something, they want it *now*. If they need to do something, they need to do it *now*. This insistence on the present can be amusing, wearing, or even nerve-racking when you're the parent of a demanding toddler. But it's a fact of very young life we can't ignore.

To a very young child, tomorrow isn't there. Since tomorrow doesn't exist for them, it's scary. Expecting them to respond to the concept of an imminent future is like asking adults to step forward into a deep, shadowy hole. Because now is all small children know, it's safe and where they want to be.

Because most adults spend the majority of their time in the past and future, we don't make a point of encouraging our children to continue living in the now. Instead, we stress future responsibility and past remorse. A single father, for instance, may spend a good part of his weekend with his children lamenting how much he misses them when he and they are apart. A well-meaning mother may worry about how the children will handle her new work schedule instead of enjoying the vacation days they have. Warns David Elkind, "By worrying about the past and future, we lose the present, and our children don't have us, even when we are around."

The following techniques and ideas, all related to the now, are designed to help you show your child that the present is a delightful place to be.

• Notice the Natural Now. Nature offers an endless array of special moments. But parents are usually too busy to notice. To refocus and notice the now, share a sunset with your child. Talk about the colors you see and the way you feel about the sky. Read "cloud pictures" aloud together. Investigate snowflakes. Crunch through autumn leaves or watch a bird balance on a tree branch. As both of you describe your sense of wonder, give the moment your complete attention. Teach your child by your example that these reflective peaceful moments are magical and meaningful.

• Stop action. Talk together about one activity that your child did that day. Ask your daughter to describe it in detail. Instead of urging her to speed up her story, commit to listening to it in entirety. Then relate something that you did and describe it in careful detail.

Or talk about what's happening at that very moment. Tell each other how you feel about what's going on right now. Maybe you hear the radio playing or a fan running. As you describe the sound, describe how that sound makes you feel. By listening in this closely focused manner, you demonstrate that you value time spent just with your child. At the same time, you illustrate how now moments serve to interrupt the pace of parental hurrying. Having made your youngster the reason for your now, there's no cause to rush.

We're so busy teaching our children to plan, to prepare, and to clean up after themselves, we forget to remind them to enjoy the present. Because parents want their older children to be responsible, they teach them to obey the clock. By the time children reach their teens, they're conditioned to clock urgency. What's more, because adults take a long-range view, we expect to find this viewpoint in teenagers. A father bemoans that his fifteen-year-old has no sense of time. A teacher asserts, "You should have thought about this ahead of time!"

Teaching your teenager to value the now can help your adolescent get in touch with himself and get the most out of all experiences. Instead of only thinking about the trip planned for August, living in the now can inspire your son to buckle down through July and concentrate on summer school. Rather than worrying about her last physics test, a focus on present time prompts your daughter to forget that past grade and tackle this exam with fresh determination.

By reintroducing the importance of the present, parents show teenagers how to put the past and future into perspective. This approach can go a long way to alleviate teenage stress. Teens need to know that the present is an appealing place, that if they deal effectively with the events in the here and now, tomorrow will take care of itself.

Don't worry that this approach encourages teenagers to be shortsighted. Teens are sophisticated enough to understand that they still need to plan.

Small children seem perfectly balanced with their sense of themselves as they move through the day. It's only when adults expect children to conform to our schedules that this delicate balance may be upset. Faced with grown-up demands, babies cry and toddlers announce firmly, "No! Me no go." These responses indicate that a child is caught uncomfortably between rhythms.

The earlier children learn to respect their own balance, the easier it is for them to maintain it as they grow older. Parents who change their philosophy of time to New Time will want to encourage their youngsters to be aware of their own rhythms and help them live comfortably within their natural range.

Here are a few ways parents can make balance and rhythm part of their children's lives. As you read through these suggestions, no doubt you'll think of other ideas.

Make time to talk!

"Don't communicate," says David Elkind. "That's too difficult. Just talk to your child." Where you talk isn't important. Talk when you're in the car or cooking dinner. Talk about the day and the natural pace you live at. If you do things quickly, tell your youngster that you are naturally a "rushing" kind of person. Ask him what kind of person he thinks he is. Then talk about how you can accommodate each other.

Plan together moments!

If you work outside the home, schedule specific times to be with your children in the early morning or evening when you won't feel stressed. Many parents find that this works best if they keep the same block of time available daily for their youngsters. Some save early morning, knowing that a premeditated cuddle from 6:20 A.M. to 6:40 A.M. feels just as good as a spontaneous hug later in the day. Others treasure a private hour before dinner to enjoy a time of closeness.

Hang out together!

Balance rushing time with "hanging-out" time. Parents often believe that every minute has to count—during the week and on weekends. When your appointment book screams "commitments" and the laundry pile rivals an ancient pyramid, coloring together may seem silly. It isn't. Often the best times together are those spent doing nothing. Parents should value hanging-out times and even doing nothing with their child.

Build a team!

Enlist your child as part of your team. Remember that you don't have to solve everything yourself. If you're feeling beleaguered, confide in your child that you're feeling upset or tired. Perhaps she may have some insights. Children often are quick to see to the heart of a matter. At the very least, you'll get sympathy. Let your child be part of your household working team. Even small children can help with dusting. Working and sharing together reinforces synchrony.

Respect your child's rhythms!

Treat your child to the same courtesy you show yourself. Parents need to recognize and allow their children their own biological rhythms. So urges Dr. Marilyn Heins, vice dean of the University of Arizona Medical School and author of *Child Care/Parent Care*. "This is part of their wonderful uniqueness

which you don't wish to change even if you could!" As soon
as possible, give children responsibility for getting themselves
up. Allow them sleep-in time on weekends without being
concerned that this habit will foster laziness.

Phase with care!

Encourage balance. Give children time to adjust to leaving
one thing and beginning another activity. Toddlers respond
well to ten-minute warnings before you plan to leave. That
way they can put all their toys away, complete a drawing, or
finish a favorite television program. Older children benefit
from the same consideration. If rushing from event to event
wears your son down, suggest that he design "cool-down"
time in his daily routine.

Anything goes!

Foster balance by allowing your younger child periods of
unstructured time. These are "anything-goes" intervals with
no appointments, no chores, and no pressure. Maybe all your
child will do during these times is bounce a ball. Instead of
rushing to organize his actions into a game, relax. Appreciate
that bouncing is what he needs to do right now. Unstructured
time slows us down and quiets us. It allows us to hear intuitive
messages that get lost in the noisier times of our day. Encouraging unstructured time gives children permission to recenter. It teaches them the value of balance in their lives.

Know your fit!

Pay attention to how your personality "fits" with your child's.
Some people are naturally flexible and have little difficulty
making quick transitions. Others are born with more rigid
personalities and naturally resist change. Power struggles may
erupt when a flexible mother comes up against a more rigid

child. If a Saturday morning filled with a mother-child swim class, followed by a visit with friends, errands, and a birthday party invigorates you but exhausts your six-year-old, aim for a more comfortable balance that fits both of you.

Permit private times!

Alone moments can restore balance. If your older child likes to be by herself behind closed doors, don't take this as a sign of rejection. Recognize that your child may need this time to readjust her rhythms. As long as her privacy doesn't interfere with family interaction, relax. And let your child do so as well.

Balancing acts

Many of the exercises suggested in chapter 6 work well for kids. Because children have fewer inhibitions, they can re-center naturally once they are shown how to do so. You can make a game of circular deep breathing (page 86). Or you may ask your daughter to imagine the "magic dial" with numbers from 1 to 10 (page 100). Explain that the number 5 means she's feeling great and all the other numbers show that something doesn't feel quite right. If she reports a number that indicates she's not feeling balanced, encourage her to explain what isn't feeling right just then.

Muscle relaxation also restores natural rhythms. Children can learn how to create and let go of tension by tightening and relaxing sets of muscles from their heads down through their toes. Many youngsters also respond well to meditation and visualization. You can appeal to their imagination by suggesting that they empty their mind of everything and fill it with a single, soothing sound. Choose any nonsense word or any word they love and concentrate for a few minutes on that sound. Meditation has a positive physiological effect because it activates alpha waves of the brain.

Value play!

Because play is nature's way of handling tension and restoring balance, make sure that your school-age child has some non-academic activities in his or her school day. Physical exercise offers an excellent outlet for balance. So do the arts. "Elective" subjects like music, art, or drama give children valuable opportunities to get in touch with their rhythms. Instead of insisting that a seventh grader take a second math course or a foreign language as an elective, you may suggest photography or band.

Helping teenagers to readjust their balance can be a special challenge. Peers and biological changes may render teens hopelessly "off the wall." Overprogrammed teenagers are especially susceptible to "PFF" (pimples, fat, and failing grades). The best cure for this condition is a balanced sense of self and time.

Talking—with lots of love and patience—can go a long way toward bringing balance into your teenager's life. Teens need to know that you value their unique rhythms. Instead of making a child feel guilty that she's not doing "enough" or complaining to him that he's doing too much, parents should become aware and respectful of their teenager's range of balance. During the teenage years it's important to encourage older children to experiment with that range. They need to push the envelope at times to test how far they can comfortably cruise before they crash.

Most will soon figure out where they like to operate. They know their priorities and their limits. Parents can help foster this awareness by talking about how everyone—including themselves—has boundaries beyond which they no longer can function comfortably.

Respecting a teenager's rhythms may be difficult for a mother who wants a room cleaned "right now." But isn't part of the challenge of raising teenagers to admit that their rhythms are different from yours and then consciously adjust to each other's balance?

"Play" is an excellent way for older children to reestablish a sense of balance by participating in the arts beyond school. Music, art, or acting classes all can give teens a sense of timelessness. Whether performing a classic fugue, reciting a sonnet, or drumming in a heavy metal band, the arts effortlessly link the past, the present, and the future.

While this next suggestion may go against the parental grain, teens do need time to zone out. Doing nothing helps teenagers refocus and regroup. In moderation, television can be chewing gum for the brain. Not only can a sitcom be an escape from daily pressures, it can also be an avenue for regaining balance. Applied sparingly and only when needed, "mindless" TV can soothe out-of-sync rhythms.

Various breathing, centering, and visualization exercises presented in chapter 6 are also excellent tools for teenagers. These techniques reopen the right side of the brain, which is active during preschool years. By the time children reach the preteens, they're almost totally dependent on left-brain input. Tuning into the right brain allows teens to hear intuitive messages, which, in turn, helps them regain natural balance.

For teens whose coping skills could use some help, biofeedback is another avenue to explore. Again, by going within to control external reactions, biofeedback techniques reinforce natural balance.

Young children do a superb job of living with purpose. They're consumed with joy as they delve into activities. They naturally march to their inner music, fascinated by themselves and focused completely on what they are doing. As you watch a toddler engrossed in a toy, the message is obvious. The child's purpose in life is to have fun—and learn in the process.

How can we, as parents, keep this vital sense of purpose alive as our children grow? When we live on purpose ourselves, time becomes a conduit for relaying this message. Having a clear sense of what we are all about allows us to understand how time fits into our life. Remember: Purpose is not synonymous with responsibility. Responsibility usually refers to what others expect us to be doing at various times.

Purpose can be explained simply to even young children. To introduce children to the concept, don't ask your children "What do you want to be when you grow up?" Inquire instead "What activities give you pleasure? What are you doing that you enjoy doing more than other activities?" Helping children to assess their interests through talking about what makes them happy or creates enthusiasm in their day is a first step toward teaching your children to live on purpose.

By teaching children to recognize what makes them happy at a point in time, parents help their children develop an understanding of the role that purpose will play in their lives and lay the framework for defining directions children will follow later.

Try some of these techniques to encourage your child to live on purpose.

• Caring activity. Help children structure more time in the day for those activities they care about. Children need to see that time can support them in their interests, that time isn't a negative factor but a positive force. This may mean eliminating a few other activities, but children can understand that as schedules get busier, trade-offs are expected. Rather than feeling that something is amiss if they can't do it all, children gain a sense of accomplishment as they see that time can support their interests.

• Affirmations. The daily affirmation mentioned in chapter 7 can be useful with elementary school and older children. Encourage children to begin the day by saying "Today I will include activities in my day that I love doing." If your child is too young to do this alone, you can help by asking "What would you really enjoy including in your day?" By inviting children to think about their day in this way, you reinforce their sense of personal power. Again, by validating purpose, you show your children that they are not a victim of time. Instead, they are convinced that they can control their day.

• Validating change. Children need to know that ideas and interests change. Purpose isn't forever. Boys and girls of all ages can benefit when parents share their own experiences with their children. Let your child know now and then that as you matured you tried out various ideas, had certain goals, and that you frequently changed your mind. Show your child that purpose isn't a single goal or a set aim, rather it's having a clear sense of who you choose to be at a certain moment in time.

• Encourage contemplation. Introduce even young children to quiet times they can use to get back in touch with who they are. Contemplative times are perfect when things don't feel right or an activity suddenly seems more difficult than fun. Make sure that an older child's schedule isn't so packed that there's no time for such reflective moments. As your child discovers them, respect their having them to themselves; these are *their* moments.

• Avoid time frames. Parents unwittingly put additional pressure on their children when they assume that youngsters should achieve within a predetermined time. This artificial pressure, coupled with the child's need for parental approval, not only sets an uncomfortable pace, it's sure to extinguish a child's concept of what he or she is all about. Respecting a youngster's purpose helps parents avoid the problems caused by packaging kids into developmental time periods. Children who grow with a strong sense of who they are usually flourish with flexible time frames that allow them to realize their own purposes rather than yours.

Decision making begins very early in our lives. As toddlers, we assert ourselves by answering "yes" or "no" to questions. As we grow older, we become more cautious with our answers. We weigh these "yeses" or "nos" within a wide parameter of feelings. We take into account the past, we condition decisions of the present with anticipated doses of the future, and we prepare decisions within the context of our environment.

By the time we reach adolescence, we often make choices according to the established decision of the day. Peer pressure can be fierce.

Again, as with purpose, your job as a parent is to teach an attitude that helps your children cultivate their power to make choices. While empowering children can be immensely gratifying, it can also be painful. It's not easy to stand by and watch your children make decisions that you disagree with. Whether it's a four-year-old's choice of a party dress or a twenty-four-year-old's choice of a mate, parents are often put to the test by their children's choices. By empowering them to design their time, however, we free them to define their lives.

• Practice free choice. Let preelementary children make simple choices like selecting the clothes they'll wear that day (appropriate for their age), what they'll eat for lunch, even what they will do most of the day. Should a child become unhappy with some of her choices, bored with a toy, or upset with a playmate, talk about this with her. Take care to respect your child's choice—even if it's one you never would have made. Remember, even if your child is disappointed in the outcome, it was still her decision.

Don't label any safe or well-intentioned choice as a mistake. Let your child know that there are no right or wrong decisions, that everyone makes choices based on the best information available at that moment. If the moment changes, as it often does, we sometimes need to change our minds. This is a natural process and is nothing to fear or be upset by. Emphasize, too, that it's also okay to wait!

• Liberate older children! After children enter school there should still be plenty of time for choosing what they will do with the remainder of their day. During the school year, consequences of time choices become especially clear. For instance, if your sixteen-year-old daughter chooses to be a cheerleader, join the Spanish language club, hold a class office, and earn money by baby-sitting fifteen hours a week, homework could suffer. This would be a good occasion to encourage her to design her schedule to support the person she chooses to be. Again, this may mean making some difficult choices as she discovers that she cannot be all things to everyone, be true to the person she chooses to be, and still make the honor roll.

• Encourage "yes" and "no"! While young children do this naturally, older children can benefit from the exercise presented in chapter 8. Walk through the exercise together. Show your son how to simplify decision making. As he becomes more comfortable with this technique and more at ease making conscious choices, he'll be less quick to follow the lead of others. Even so, give him latitude to change his mind. Let him know that even consciously made choices are not irrevocable. Ideas, feelings, and circumstances change. The good news is that as we become proficient at making conscious choices, our flexibility and tolerance increases. When we no longer agonize over our choices, we make decisions more easily.

Once your child becomes comfortable with conscious choice, you may suggest other ways this technique can be used. For instance, if your teenage daughter is feeling swamped, she might need to do a "housecleaning" of what's doable versus what's essential. As she runs through her list of commitments, allowing herself to answer "yes" or "no" to each, she'll discover that conscious choice can provide insight as to which items on her agenda are contributing extra stress.

If your elementary-age son is spending an inordinate amount of time in front of the television, you might walk him through an exercise in which he mentally parades all the things he likes to do—including television—in front of himself. As he sees each activity, he makes a conscious choice about whether or not he chooses to do this. Once he has his list of things he likes to do in addition to watching television, help him design his time to include some of these other activities.

By using conscious choice in this manner, children avoid being locked into doing only what adults demand of them. Because youngsters have the opportunity to make many of their own choices, they "invest" in their decisions. This, in turn, inspires these children to be more diligent when carrying out their commitments.

RHYTHM AND SCHOOL BELLS

Parents form the first line of offense, but schools must also share responsibility for shaping a child's concept of time. Historically, a school's temporal organization was determined by the group it served. Where formal schools existed in agricultural societies, the school year was organized to allow students time off during planting and harvesting seasons. In industrial societies, schools historically are run by the clock. Although we're in the midst of the postindustrial period, schools still obey clock time.

At first glance, most schools look remarkably alike. Nearly all elementary and high schools run on clock time. With few exceptions, students are expected to follow a daily schedule. Class periods are set. Students are penalized for being tardy. They're punished by being kept late, or they're rewarded with "free time." And everyone—teachers and kids—looks forward to time off.

But as children know—and perceptive parents can readily discover—different schools "feel different." They can have rhythms as distinctive as an individual's rhythms. Schools march to their own beats and keep time to their own clocks.

Even more important, time and timing is critical to the learning process. Time values permeate a school, and a teacher's approach to time can dramatically affect how a child thinks about, absorbs, and learns to restructure information. The challenge for parents, then, is to learn how to "sight-read" these rhythms.

How can you as a parent get a sense of how your child's school values time? Begin by observing the school and classroom and asking questions. Starting at the district level, inquire about the district's mission statement or educational objective for students. Ask about the value this district assigns to time. How is the daily schedule divided? Is there a complete focus on clockwork organization? Are class periods ever rearranged? Does the district schedule allow flexibility for unusual field trips or special speakers? How rigid or casual is the district about deviating from routine? What is the absentee policy? By asking these kinds of questions, you can get a sense of how the district regards time.

Next, talk directly with your child's teacher. Ask the teacher how he or she feels about—and therefore "teaches" about—time. Is punctuality paramount? Is flexibility encouraged or tolerated? If a child hasn't completed something and it's time to move on to another subject, how does the teacher handle this? Are children often given extra time to finish assignments or projects? Are they encouraged to hurry along to keep up? Does the teacher make a point of assuring students that they can go back to a particular activity and finish it later?

What about the school day? Does the school emphasize calendric time? Are holidays and seasonal differences celebrated? Does the school's curriculum support a cyclical or organic view of time, introducing students to a subject in one grade and then presenting it again in more depth later?

How is the school's approach to time reflected in its philosophy of child development? At either the district or teacher level, ask about how the curriculum is presented. Is one method generally followed? Or is flexibility encouraged? Having first determined the normal patterns of child development, some districts establish a district-wide policy as to how classes will be taught. Others may follow the traditional policy for one subject, but then rearrange the classroom schedule when presenting another topic. Parents should make a point of knowing how the curriculum is taught so that they are comfortable with the school's temporal rhythm.

Pay attention to pacing as well. Some educational institutions subscribe to "more is better." Using the normal developmental stages that the majority of children go through, one school may pride itself on covering many topics thoroughly but quickly throughout the year, while another may take a more individual approach and plan accordingly. Then, too, one institution may adhere strictly to a mechanistic view of time where the clock is king, while another school, although also working by the clock, may take a more flexible view of scheduling and attendance. If you're not comfortable with how your child's school presents this mix, or perhaps more important, if your child is not comfortable with it, there are opportunities—PTA open-house evenings, appointments with teachers and administration (including guidance counselors)—to express your discomfort and try to effect changes.

New Time will grow with your child. Youngsters who approach planning their days from a perspective of their needs and choices develop a strong sense of self and a positive attitude about time. They become empowered individuals. Independent and interconnected, New Time students can meet the future confidently.

DESIGNING FAMILY TIME

Designing time from the inside out is something the whole family can share. As families live in the now, respect balance, work and play with purpose, activate conscious choice, and synchronize with others in the household, time becomes an asset instead of a liability. Family time and space is at a premium in today's world. In a recent *USA Today* poll, 47 percent of those surveyed felt that their life had become busier in the past year. Asked what gets shortchanged when life is most hectic, 71 percent of the respondents answered household chores, 52 percent said television, 46 percent said friends, and 41 percent said family. Only 7 percent pointed to their jobs.

By empowering individuals, Inner Time can encourage family cohesion. In a well-managed family, just as in a productive company, every person is aware of his or her own power and yet comes together willingly. At times, one parent's or a child's needs may dominate over needs of others, but the power balance shifts continually. Each person in the family feels connected to the others not only because of the accident of birth, but because each appreciates that together they create a synergy of love and spirit.

MORE THINGS YOU CAN DO

• Be flexible! When the pace gets too hectic or arrangements demand inordinate amounts of effort, flexibility is a family's best friend. Relatively few things really must be done that day—at a specific time. Most of us have more latitude in our days and nights than we suspect.

• So it's a zoo! Don't panic if, occasionally, your household's "now" becomes a zoo. Even the most attuned and organized homes run into snags. Perfection is an ideal; it's not a realistic goal. Besides, since families are microcosms of society, home is a great place to practice "fight or flight," to rehearse your physiological response to stress. That way you are better prepared to handle pressures in the real world. Like a vaccination, a little family stress doesn't hurt long.

• Be tradition-minded! Whether baking a special cake to celebrate family birthdays or making an occasion out of seeing the autumn leaves, let now moments punctuate your family present. Such moments create an awareness of temporal continuity and connectedness that our everyday existence can't supply. Dr. Heins insists that these traditional moments serve as benchmarks for children. Benchmarks, she knows, make useful furniture in homes.

• Pace your now! Children of different ages have different paces. Consider your child's pace when planning a family outing. Some outings are fine for everyone; others are not. Instead of making one full-day trip to an amusement park with a ten- and a five-year-old in tow, treat each child separately to an afternoon at the park. Not only will each enjoy the experience more, but you'll become a part of each child's special now in the process.

• Taste now at mealtimes! Some families accentuate the now by eating breakfast together on Sunday mornings. They use this time to talk about personal experiences or world events. Other busy families make a point of eating dinner together two evenings a week, catching each other up on what they're doing and giving support to each other.

• Spotlight vacations! Some families take an annual ski trip where they spend 95 percent of their time together— skiing, eating, playing games, and talking. While such vacations can be magic, they can also be manic. Children quarrel. Parents fight. Motels are dirty. Boats break down. Wise families don't save all their now moments for a single two-week stretch. They scatter meaningful moments liberally throughout the year. A hot game of Pictionary or an evening spent together browsing in a bookstore can inject a healthy breather into a frenzied schedule and mitigate the hassles of daily life.

• Maintain family balance! Be open about the times when you are not in balance. Let your children know how you feel when your rhythms are not in sync with others in the family and encourage them to express their own feelings. Everyone can cope better with shifts in energy and concentration when each person knows that an ebb and flow is natural.

• Identify family goals! Be as specific or general as you wish, but take the time to talk openly about the values your family holds dear and the relationship you would like to foster. Some situations naturally encourage this kind of family soul-searching. For instance, if you are considering having a foreign exchange student come to live with you for a year, your family will need to talk openly about what each person hopes to gain by this experience. At the same time, parents and children should voice their fears and hesitations. By entering into this introspective discussion, each member of the family becomes aware of the path the others are following at this time.

Frequently family counselors recommend that families in trouble develop goals together. This can be successful if the family doesn't become too structured in its approach and if the joint goals are compatible with those of everyone in the household. As you listen to each other, it may be necessary to remind everyone that there are no "right" or "wrong" answers to purpose.

• Choose family first! Making conscious choices within the family means actively valuing each other as much as we value our work. Making conscious decisions that support the family teaches children the value of home.

• Make household jobs a family affair! Instead of arbitrarily assigning chores or, worse, being a martyr and trying to handle everything yourself, let each family member select the tasks he or she prefers to do. For more complex choices, rely on the Inner Time technique of yes/no and use the three self-centering questions. While complicated decisions are never easy, taking a Taoist approach diffuses emotionalism and helps everyone see the choice more clearly. Successful family decisions result when everyone tunes into his or her intuitive message center besides listening to the logical self. Phrasing any question so that it can be answered by a "yes" or "no" can simplify even the most complex situation.

Of course, the best reason for teaching children about New Time is to equip them to face the future. The kindergarten class of 1990 is the high school class of the year 2002. In the twenty-first century, our sense of time and self will be tested beyond our imagination. Children who grow up comfortable with their own rhythms and who feel connected to the world around them will be in the best position to adapt effortlessly to the challenges that lie ahead.

25

New Time
and the Coming Century

Every transformation ... has rested on a new metaphysical and
ideological base; or rather upon the deeper stirrings and in-
tuitions whose rationalized expression takes the form of a new
picture of the cosmos and the nature of man.

Lewis Mumford,
The Transformation of Man

What's so special about today's concern for the year 2000 and
beyond? Beyond the circumstance of turning into a new mil-
lennium, doesn't each new century herald a time of reflection,
moments for taking stock of where we've been and wondering
where we are going?

The difference this time, say futurists, is that never before
have the forces of change been as concentrated, the pace as
frenetic, or the issues so globally intertwined. It's as if we're
poised at a crossroads as we approach the new century. One
road, dedicated to acceleration, is the familiar fast track. The
other, committed to separating ourselves from that track, is
aimed at getting us off the merry-go-round. This second
avenue promises a less conventional but more intimate voyage.
As the twentieth century concludes, we have a unique opportunity—some would say an obligation—to examine these
roads and make our choice.

Already dubbed by some the Age of Acceleration, the
new era will ride the jet stream of the past few decades. But
while the rate of speed is impressive, the force of change
carries the greater impact. The speed and scope of change

strains our comprehension. Just think. In the last twenty years we've witnessed the end of the Industrial Age and the beginning of a transformation to a global Information Age. We've experienced complete revolutions in knowledge and recorded far-reaching upheaval on the social front. We've created entire new systems of comunications and invented new modes of transportation that together have shrunk the globe to ever-smaller dimensions.

Largely as a result of these technological advances, we see evidence of global consciousness everywhere and in everything. Today we eat, think, dress, live, and sleep internationally in a world as influenced by the East as by Europe, and we rarely give our global purview more than a passing thought.

As we careen toward the twenty-first century, global change is a given. Look at what is already happening.

• Politically we are fast becoming a global village. Thanks to breakthroughs in communication and transportation, we are identifying worldwide problems.

• Ecologically, the earth is being fused into a planetary state. Today a vast fire or oil spill in a remote location is not an isolated occurrence. Spewed ash and spilled oil let loose anywhere on this planet in heavy doses are rightly seen as threats to survival. Within weeks and sometimes days, ecological repercussions ripple throughout the world.

• Economically, we know at last that we are all in this together. When one money market coughs, the others feel the chill—anywhere on the planet. As the fortunes of multinational corporations shift, shock waves often reverberate through all major continents. The rapid ascendancies of Far Eastern national economies and their penetration of Western markets has been astounding.

On the national front as well, change is endemic. Demographically, the United States is undergoing a major population shift. On the one hand, the nation is growing steadily older. Once maligned, middle age is fashionable; old age, long a brief stop on the road to heaven, is becoming a destination resort. At the same time, the male-female ratio is swinging 180 degrees. Where women have been the majority during the last fifty years, by the turn of the century demographers expect an excess of eligible men. Sociologists can only guess at the long-term consequences of these shifts.

What do all of these societal changes mean for us as individuals? Despite—or perhaps because of—these sweeping physical, political, economic, and environmental variables, we are today experiencing a universal heightening of individual awareness. Because change affects each of us personally, we are seeing an overwhelming desire to get in touch with who we are and *why* we are. Many of us are undergoing various degrees of personal transformation. As a result, according to recent research, the 1990s person is a different breed from the 1970s or even the 1980s individual.

Information compiled by trend-watchers Yankelovich, Clancy, and Shulman recently described and labeled the 1990s person the "Neo-Traditionalist." This individual synthesizes many of the values of the 1950s but puts them in the context of the experiences of the 1960s, 1970s, and 1980s. Neo-Traditionalists care about a strong work ethic, individual responsibility, a loving family, and a secure home, but at the same time they remain vitally concerned about their inner selves and committed to fulfilling their emotional and spiritual needs.

Happily, the Neo-Traditionalist is searching for many of the same qualities that underlie the philosophy of the "Tao of Time." As you begin your journey to New Time, it may help you to know that you are in step with the 1990s and beyond, and that others—such as the many successful businesspeople you have met in this book—are walking this same path toward personal fulfillment.

Here are some characteristics culled from the Yankelovich

report that are common to Neo-Traditionalists. As you'll see, these traits are in harmony with the Tao and in keeping with the new way of time.

• NTs are actively searching for a point of equilibrium.
• They are concerned with filling their lives with inherent value and meaning.
• They care about personal virtues and aren't embarrassed to speak openly about them.
• They yearn to streamline their lives. Where the traditional person of the 1950s wanted to keep life simple, do what was on the approved list, and to approach things in their correct order, NTs have moved beyond those limits. A 1990s individual believes "I can do anything I want to, but I choose *not* to do everything." So NTs set priorities.
• NTs accept the idea of "good enough." They aren't driven to give that last 5 percent to attain perfection. In touch with themselves, they don't subscribe to others' definitions of "ideal."
• NTs search for simplicity. They don't want to add complexity to their lives in order to make changes. Some, like Deborah Madison, founding chef of The Greens restaurant, physically leave high-pressure jobs and fast-track locations to establish smaller businesses in less frantic towns and even rural communities. They forgo the trappings of success if they suspect personal problems in trying to attain those trappings.
• NTs lavish time and energy on personal needs and desires, spiritual values, and communication. However, where the 1950s person touted self-denial and the 1970s person was into self-indulgence, the 1990s NT seeks self-control. NTs want control of their time and their money—not for the sake of control, but so that they can enjoy splurges. Above all, NTs are honest in their desires and communication.
• They take a bit more time to make decisions. NTs aren't driven to rush out and try everything new immediately.
• They have adjusted their planning values. Although the

traditional 1950s person lived in the future and the person of the 1970s lived for the moment, Neo-Traditionalists acknowledge the impact of change. Some planning is necessary, but they won't worry too far into the future.

DECELERATION AND INDIVIDUALITY

For the last century, as we've climbed the acceleration spiral, we've been told that if only we can learn to manage our time, we can control our lives. Such was the prevailing wisdom. Only now do we understand that we've had it backward. By controlling our lives, we create our time.

Inner Time is attuned to the 1990s and beyond because it celebrates individuality. Unlike other time management methods, this new way of time is intensely personal in design. It exhorts us to find and savor our individual rhythms, points of balance that syndicated newspaper columnist Ellen Goodman calls "small personal pockets of time." It urges us to pay attention to our intuitive selves. It reminds us that there is no system that can show us how to do it all. Rather, Inner Time gently counsels us that there is always time for whatever we choose to do.

By accepting the premise that change starts within each of us, Inner Time prepares us to live in the global society. When we are connected to Inner Time, the wide-sweeping forces of global change seem less threatening. At the same time, Inner Time techniques challenge us to discover more about ourselves. Those who follow Inner Time quickly learn that they are more than the sum of their biological clocks, more than a sequence of time intervals, more than a calendar or appointment book or digital readout.

Above all, following the four Taoist-inspired steps encourages us to set and maintain our own pace in the midst of an ever-accelerating world. Living with intentional timeless nows removes us from the speeding spiral by putting us back in touch with the meaning of the everyday occurrences in our lives. Focusing on the now obliges us to confront small segments of time—immediate moments that we often skip over in our rush to plan for the next event. Happily, we discover that by paying attention to the present, we often see the future more clearly.

Balance gives us the option of indulging in different speeds. Once we know our rhythms, should we decide to rush crazily for a period of time, we can do so knowing that we can always rein in and return to a more comfortable and natural pace. Thus, balance affords us the ability to decelerate or accelerate at will.

Living on purpose keeps us connected, so no matter how wide-sweeping the changes or fast-moving the spiral, we never feel that we are at the mercy of events. Instead of feeling helplessly caught up in a world that whirls by too fast, living on purpose gives us a sense of "place" that we can carry with us no matter what is going on around us.

Finally, conscious choice intensifies our personal power. Knowing that we always have the option to move ahead with the pace and direction of an event or activity, stop it, or wait to make a decision on it gives us a measure of control that functions apart from the velocity of the circumstance. In addition, the insight we gain from using the yes/no Inner Time technique helps us see how we can simplify our lives, which in turn offers yet another way to gain a measure of control over our always-changing environment.

Most of us won't suddenly become comfortable with time. The process is a natural unfolding. At first, as you practice the visualizations described in this book and begin designing your time, it will be enough for you to achieve a measure of peace in your day, the direct result of your having gained a sense of order and completion that previously eluded you. However, as you continue exploring this approach to time, you'll find that you begin to move easily from the active to the receptive mode of visualization. At this point, you'll enter

another level of awareness, one in which there is a consistent
and profound sense of knowing that occurs naturally without
your having to actively create scenes to stimulate this knowledge.

Like the Tao, this philosophy of time elicits many layers
of understanding. Although you may begin using the deceleration program with a clear sense of what you want to
accomplish with it, as you continue practicing its techniques
you'll find that your needs expand. Where once you measured
success by the number of highlights you accomplished in a
day, you notice now that you are more concerned about your
sense of personal satisfaction—gauged by your sense of connectedness and direction. What's happening is that your inner
growth is accelerating at the same time that, outwardly, you
are settling into a more comfortable pace.

The intellectual part of you may still be wondering how
you can prove that this new way of time is really working
for you. Because New Time depends so much on your own
personal reactions, no blanket scientific experiments can be
devised to test it. As with any program that involves self-
exploration, a degree of faith must be factored in. However,
you can run some checks yourself. Here are three questions
to ask yourself to help you clarify your reaction to this program.

• Do you intuitively feel this way of time is working for
you even though you may not be able to demonstrate it? Is
this a consistent feeling? When you find yourself drifting
away from these techniques, can you pull yourself back into
Inner Time at will?

• Have you noticed this way of approaching time carrying
over to other parts of your life? Think of specific instances
of conflict that the Inner Time techniques have been useful
in resolving.

• Can you imagine how the world would be if everyone
behaved in accordance with this way of time? Does this seem

plausible? It should. Why? Because the new way of time is contagious. Once set free, Inner Time could become an epidemic. To spot rampant deceleration, be on the lookout for any of these signs and symptoms in people you interact with.

- A conspicuous ability to enjoy each moment
- A tendency to think and act spontaneously rather than react to the clock
- A noticeable inability to worry
- An increased level of tolerance
- Irresistible feelings of connectedness with others and with nature
- A marked propensity to let things happen naturally instead of forcing things to occur
- Smiling and laughing more often
- Nurturing meaningful relationships
- Being unconcerned with calendars and clocks— maybe even going without a watch
- Suddenly appearing at ease
- Being able to wait without undue agitation
- Being less concerned about maintaining "control"

As you grow in your understanding of time and yourself, this book will continue to take on new meaning. With each step you take, each time you read it, you will discover new insights. This process is not complicated or difficult so long as you have an overwhelming desire to let go of those old customs of managing time that confined you and restricted your personal growth. Letting go is vital to gaining trust. With trust comes simplicity.

Simplicity is essential for the future. In the past, we've made time so complicated that we no longer can comprehend it. In the coming century we must simplify the way we approach and use our time.

By giving us the go-ahead to tap into our own inner guidance system, this simplified decelerated method offers us a way in rather than a way out of traditional time-pressured dilemmas. Armed with an inward-bound philosophy, we discover that we have a choice. We can stay on the merry-go-round as it continues to accelerate, or we can step off and set our own pace. In making this choice, we position ourselves to make the transition from the man-driven programs we've been using during the last one hundred years to a spirit-driven approach that will reinforce the cadence of the coming century. We will realize the "Tao of Time."

SUGGESTED READINGS

(by chapter)

CHAPTER 1. TIME MANAGEMENT AS A LIFE ART

Dossey, Larry. *Space, Time, and Medicine*. Boulder: Shambhala Press, 1982. *A thought-provoking look beyond our traditional concepts of the universe and the role of time.*

Gardet, L. *Cultures and Time*. Paris: The Unesco Press, 1976. *The influence of time in various cultures.*

Guitton, Jean. *Man in Time*. Notre Dame, IND: University of Notre Dame Press, 1966. *The evolution of time and man; a historical and philosophical perspective.*

Hall, Edward T. *The Dance of Life: The Other Dimension of Time*. New York: Anchor/Doubleday, 1983. *An anthropological view of time.*

Hawking, Stephen W. *A Brief History of Time*. New York: Bantam, 1988. *A classic introduction to today's most important and scientific ideas about the cosmos.*

Jantsch, Erich. *The Self-Organizing Universe*. New York: Pergamon Press, 1984. *The scientific and human implications of the emerging paradigm of evolution.*

Rifkin, Jeremy. *Time Wars*. New York: Henry Holt, 1987. *A well-documented work about the nature of time and our personal and political relationship to it.*

Whitrow, G. J. *The Natural Philosophy of Time*. Oxford: Oxford University Press, 1980. *A description of time in nature and its relation to the plant and animal worlds.*

CHAPTER 2. CLASSIC THEORY REVISITED

Barrett, Ross. *Executive Time Control Program*. Englewood Cliffs, NJ: Prentice-Hall, 1965. *Traditional time management techniques.*

Bennis, W. G. *Organizational Development*. Reading, MA: Addison-Wesley, 1969. *A classic work describing all structures of an organization.*

Bliss, Edwin C. *Getting Things Done: The ABC's of Time Management*. New York: Scribner, 1976. *Traditional time management techniques.*

Capra, Fritjof. *The Turning Point*. New York: Simon and Schuster, 1982. *An essential guide for anyone interested in the role of science and metascience in our contemporary culture.*

Carlson, S. *Executive Behavior*. Stockholm: Strombergs, 1951. *A classic study of top management conduct.*

Cooper, Joseph. *How to Get More Done in Less Time*. New York: Doubleday, 1971. *Traditional time management techniques.*

Drucker, Peter. *The Effective Executive*. New York: Harper & Row, 1967. *Compilation of clasic suggestions to help the executive operate more efficiently.*

Ferner, Jack. *Successful Time Management*. New York: John Wiley & Sons, 1980. *A self-teaching time management program.*

Forbes, Rosalind. *Corporate Stress*. New York: Doubleday, 1979. *The effects of stress on individuals within an organization and the resulting changes within the corporate culture.*

Jennings, Eugene E. *The Mobile Manager*. New York: McGraw-Hill, 1971. *Concerns of and suggestions for managers who need to remain effective while moving in and out of several environments.*

Laird, Donald A. and Eleanor C. Laird. *The Techniques of Delegating.* New York: McGraw-Hill, 1957. *Traditional time management in the art of delegation.*

Lakein, Alan. *How to Get Control of Your Time and Your Life.* New York: Signet Book/New American Library, 1973. *Traditional time management techniques.*

LeGoff, Jacques. *Time, Work, and Culture in the Middle Ages.* Chicago: The University of Chicago Press, 1980. *A historical perspective of schedules and clocks in the workplace during the Middle Ages.*

McCay, James T. *The Management of Time.* Englewood Cliffs, NJ: Prentice-Hall, 1973. *Traditional time management techniques.*

Macey, Samuel L. *Clocks and the Cosmos.* Hamden, Connecticut: Archon Books, 1980. *The role of the clock in shaping Western consciousness and culture.*

MacKenzie, R. Alec. *The Time Trap.* New York: McGraw-Hill, 1972. *Traditional time management techniques.*

Quinones, Ricardo J. *The Renaissance Discovery of Time.* Cambridge: Harvard University Press, 1972. *The effects of time on the Renaissance culture.*

Sayles, Leonard R. *Leadership.* New York: McGraw-Hill, 1979. *An excellent work describing all aspects of a "leader."*

Scott, Dru. *How to Put More Time in Your Life.* New York: Rawson Wade Publishers, 1980. *The psychological effects of time on the individual, with traditional time management techniques.*

Steiner, George A. *Strategic Planning: What Every Manager Must Know.* New York: Free Press, 1979. *An in-depth look at the pros and cons of planning and directing strategies within an organization.*

Taylor, Frederick. *The Principles of Scientific Management.* New York: W. W. Norton, 1947. *Introduction to the methods of the scientific management movement of the Industrial Revolution.*

Townsend, Robert. *Up The Organization.* New York: Knopf, 1970. *An ABC survival manual for corporations.*

Webber, Ross A. *Management: Basic Elements of Managing Organizations.* Homewood, ILL: Richard D. Irwin, 1979. *A step-by-step description of the fundamentals of management.*

Webber, Ross A. *Time Is Money.* New York: Free Press, 1980. *Traditional time management techniques.*

Winston, Stephanie. *The Organized Executive.* New York: W. W. Norton, 1983. *Traditional time management.*

CHAPTER 3. THE TAO AND TIME

Capra, Fritjof. *The Tao of Physics.* Boulder: Shambhala Press, 1975. *An exploration of the parallels between modern physics and Eastern mysticism.*

Crichton, Michael. *Travels.* New York: Alfred A. Knopf, 1988. *A best-selling novelist's account of his "inner" and "outer" adventures of self and life.*

Ferguson, Marilyn. *The Aquarian Conspiracy.* Los Angeles: Tarcher, 1980. *A provocative guide to personal and social transformation in the 1980s.*

Heider, John. *The Tao of Leadership.* New York: Bantam, 1986. *Simple advice on how to be the very best leader.*

Legge, James. *Tao Te Ching: The Writings of Chuang-Tzu.* Taipei: Ch'eng-Wen Publishing, 1969. *The philosophical translations of the Tao-te Ching.*

Maurer, Herrymon. *Tao: The Way of the Ways.* New York: Schocken Books, 1985. *Descriptive passages with some translation of the Tao.*

Meerloo, Joost A. M. *Along the Fourth Dimension.* New York: The John Day Company, 1970. *A philosophical and cultural perspective of time.*

Peat, F. David. *Synchronicity: The Bridge Between Matter and Mind.* New York: Bantam, 1987. *An exploration of the nature of energy, time, chance, causality, and coincidence.*

Rawlence, Christopher. *About Time.* London: Jonathan Cape,

1985. *An anthropological, psychological, and philosophical description of time and culture.*

Reifler, Sam. *I Ching: A New Interpretation for Modern Times.* New York: Bantam, 1974. *A contemporary translation of the sixty-four hexagrams of the I Ching.*

Siv, R. G. H. *Chi: A Neo-Taoist Approach to Life.* Cambridge: MIT Press, 1974. *A philosophical discussion of taoist premises and their application to daily living.*

Toben, Bob and Fred Alan Wolf. *Space-Time and Beyond.* New York: Bantam, 1983. *A unique word and picture guide to understanding the new physics.*

Wing, R. L. *The Tao of Power.* Garden City, NY: Doubleday, 1986. *A new translation of Lao Tzu's classic guide to leadership, influence, and excellence.*

CHAPTER 5. WEEK ONE: LIVING IN THE NOW

Borysenko, Joan, Ph.D. *Minding the Body, Mending the Mind.* New York: Bantam, 1988. *A guide to a new understanding of illness and health that shows how each of us can take an active role in healing ourselves.*

Fishel, Ruth. *Learning to Live in the Now.* Pompano Beach, FL: Health Communications, 1988. *A personal guide to promote self-knowledge and awareness of the here and now of our lives.*

Ray, Michael and Rochelle Myers. *Creativity in Business.* Garden City, NY: Doubleday, 1986. *Offers new ways to look at business through simple guidelines for unlocking the creative essence in us.*

Roman, Sanaya. *Living With Joy.* Tiburon, CA: H. J. Kramer, 1986. *A metaphysical work outlining keys to personal power and spiritual transformation.*

CHAPTER 6. WEEK TWO: GOING WITHIN FOR BALANCE

Ayensu, Edward S. and Philip Whitfield. *The Rhythms of Life.* New York: Crown Publishers, 1982. *A sociological and psychological view of how the universe "runs."*

Chia, Mantak. *Awaken Healing Energy Through the Tao.* New York: Aurora Press, 1983. *A treasury of ancient, profound knowledge of subtle energy patterns in the human body.*

Perry, Susan and Jim Dawson. *The Secrets Our Body Clocks Reveal.* New York: Rawson Associates, 1988. *How to tune into your body rhythms for peak performance.*

Trivers, Howard. *The Rhythm of Being.* New York: Philosophic Library, 1985. *A philosophical look at personal rhythms: "What makes us tick."*

Zerubavel, Eviatar. *Hidden Rhythms: Schedules and Calendars in Social Life.* Chicago: University of Chicago Press, 1981. *A sociological look at the way we organize individually as well as collectively.*

CHAPTER 7. WEEK THREE: LIVING ON PURPOSE

Frankl, Victor. *Man's Search for Meaning.* New York: Washington Square Press, 1959. *A psychological and philosophical classic about one man's search for meaning in the midst of adversity, with psychosocial implications for all.*

Peck, M. Scott. *The Road Less Traveled.* New York: Touchstone, 1978. *Integrates traditional psychological and spiritual insights to show how to achieve serenity and fullness in your life.*

Sinetar, Marsha. *Do What You Love . . . the Money Will Follow.* New York: Paulist Press, 1987. *A practical approach for those seeking to unify their life and work.*

Wilbur, Ken. *No Boundary.* Boulder: Shambhala Press, 1981. *A comprehensive guide to psychologies and therapies from both Western and Eastern sources to help individuals with personal growth.*

CHAPTER 8. WEEK FOUR: CONSCIOUS CHOICE AS A LIFE FORCE

Carlzon, Jan. *Moments of Truth.* New York: Harper & Row, 1989. *A model for management in the New Age, taking a* bold approach to meeting the demands of today's consumer-driven economy.

Roberts, Wes, Ph.D. *Leadership Secrets of Attila the Hun*. New York: Warner Books, 1987. *Principles and insights about successful leadership.*

Roman, Sanaya. *Personal Power Through Awareness*. Tiburon, CA: H. J. Kramer, 1986. *A metaphysical approach to enhance family life, daily work, and relationships.*

CHAPTER 11. SCHEDULING

Schreiber-Servan, Jean-Louis. *The Art of Time*. New York: Addison-Wesley, 1988. *Reflective thoughts about one's management of time.*

CHAPTER 18. MEETINGS, APPOINTMENTS, DEADLINES

Waitley, Denis and Robert Tucker. *Winning the Innovation Game*. Old Tappan, NJ: Fleming H. Revell Company, 1986. *Self-improvement message to prepare for and effectively deal with the challenges of today's business.*

CHAPTER 22. ADJUSTING TO OTHERS

Mornell, Pierre. *Thank God It's Monday, or How to Prevent Success from Ruining Your Marriage*. New York: Bantam, 1985. *Practical solutions to marriage and other life problems brought about by the stresses of success.*

CHAPTER 24. THE NEXT GENERATION: TEACHING YOUR CHILDREN ABOUT NEW TIME

Elkind, David. *The Hurried Child, Growing Up Too Fast Too Soon*. New York: Addison-Wesley, 1981. *Pointed discussion about the effect of societal "push" and the resulting stress on our children.*

Heins, Marilyn, M.D. and Anne Seiden. *Child Care/Parent Care*. Garden City, NY: Doubleday, 1987. *A practical, readable and complete guide to raising the modern child; written by professionals who are also mothers.*

Piaget, Jean. *The Child's Conception of Time.* New York: Basic Books, 1969. *Scientific study of the developmental stages a child goes through in comprehending time.*

Scharf, Diana, Ph.D. and Pam Hait. *Studying Smart.* New York: Harper & Row, 1985. *Practical time management system for high school and college-age students.*

CHAPTER 25. NEW TIME AND THE COMING CENTURY

Capra, Fritjof. *Uncommon Wisdom.* New York: Simon and Schuster, 1988. *Lively discussions of contemporary ideas of science, metaphysics, religion, philosophy, and health.*

Davis, Stanley M. *Future Perfect.* New York: Addison Wesley, 1987. *Intriguing discussion about the relationship of time and business, including a meaningful model for managing in the new economy.*

Devall, Bill and George Sessions. *Deep Ecology: Living as if Nature Matters.* Salt Lake City: Peregrine Smith Books, 1985. *Informative presentation about humankind and the environment.*

Granberg-Michaelson, Wesley. *A Worldly Spirituality: A Call to Take Care of the Earth.* San Francisco: Harper & Row, 1984. *Discussion of the world in crisis, particularly the environment.*

Harman, Willis, Ph.D. *Global Mind Change.* Indianapolis: Knowledge Systems, Inc., 1988. *A thought-provoking discussion about the revolutionary developments in Western scientific thought and philosophy of science.*

Kidder, Rushworth M. *An Agenda for the 21st Century.* Cambridge: MIT Press, 1987. *Interviews with some of the world's most compelling thinkers about the major issues facing humanity in the twenty-first century.*

Krishnamurti, J. and Dr. David Bohm. *The Ending of Time.* New York: Harper & Row, 1985. *Penetrating dialogues between a spiritual leader and a renowned physicist about the fundamental issues of existence.*

Mumford, Lewis. *The Transformations of Man.* New York:

Harper Brothers, 1956. *A sociological classic about man's transitional phases throughout human history.*
Turkle, Sherry. *The Second Self: Computers and the Human Spirit.* New York: Simon and Schuster, 1984. *Sociological views about the high-tech world, the people immersed in the technology, and their race against time.*
Weber, Renee. *Dialogues with Scientists and Sages: The Search for Unity.* New York: Rutledge & Kegan Paul, 1986. *Contemporary scientists and mystics share their views on time, space, matter, energy, consciousness, and our place within the universe.*